P.23

THOMAS MORE

Utopia

Crofts Classics

THOMAS MORE

Utopia

TRANSLATED AND EDITED BY

H. V. S. Ogden

UNIVERSITY OF MICHIGAN

AHM Publishing Corporation
Arlington Heights, Illinois 60004

ISBN: 0-88295-062-2
(Formerly 0-390-23185-1)

Library of Congress Card Number: 49-11368

PRINTED IN THE UNITED STATES OF AMERICA
7128
Thirty-eighth Printing

Contents

Introduction

Sir Thomas More was beheaded because he would not swear an oath accepting King Henry VIII as Supreme Head of the Church. As he laid his head upon the block, it is reported that he "bade the executioner stay until he had removed aside his beard, saying that *that* had never committed any treason." True or not, the remark reflects a characteristic side of More's personality, and one which finds clear expression in *Utopia*. His humanist friends called it *festivitas,* a sort of cheerful irony and playfulness in speech and demeanor, stemming partly from his disposition and partly from his deep conviction that it is man's duty to live cheerfully and as far as possible delightfully. The name *Utopia* itself is an example. It means "nowhere" (*ou topos*), and the other proper names in the book are in the same vein. Aside from the names and the patently comic incidents (like the account of the Anemolian ambassadors or the incubation of chickens), there is an undercurrent of humor which repeatedly breaks through in a word or phrase, unobtrusively and sometimes unnoticed.

At the same time *Utopia* is profoundly serious. Among other things it is a social satire. The comic spirit pervades some of the satire, for example the description of the French King's council meeting. Oftener it gives way to pathos or indignation, as it does in the bitter account of the families displaced by the greedy sheep-owners or in the fierce attacks on the idle rich who exploit the commonwealth in their own interest. Passages such as these, along with the communism of the Utopians, have made the book popular with modern revolutionaries, who read it as a document of social protest.

More, however, was interested in a deeper revolution than a

shift of power from one class to another or a change in form of government. He believed that the only true revolution is moral, and that changing institutions is of small value unless the new institutions produce good men and good women. At bottom *Utopia* is a book on ethics. It is an attempt to project Christian ethical values into a concrete social system. More is exploring the practical possibilities of attaining the good life among a people who wholeheartedly pursue the moral virtues of Christianity. Few writers have brought to the task a like combination of worldly success and practical experience, of spiritual insight and moral sensibility, and of intellectual detachment and discernment.

More makes no concessions to wishful-thinking about human nature. The Utopians are not naturally good, and the whole system is designed to safeguard them from the effects of human sinfulness, especially pride. The denunciation of pride near the end of Book II sums up the ethical values of the whole book in much the same way that the passage on pride at the end of Book IV of *Gulliver's Travels* sums up Swift's ethical thought.

Utopia deals primarily with ethics, not religion. But More insists that ethics must be grounded on religion, and the thought of the book is thoroughly Christian. The similarity between the religion of the Utopians and the deism of the seventeenth and eighteenth centuries is misleading. More does not look ahead to deists like Lord Herbert of Cherbury, but back to St. Paul: "For when the Gentiles, which have not the law, do by nature the things contained in the law, these having not the law, are a law unto themselves: Which shew the work of the law written in their hearts, their conscience also bearing witness, and their thought the mean while accusing or else excusing one another" (Romans ii: 14-15). The Utopians are guided by reason, i.e. "the law of nature." But they are not deists, as their priesthood, their liturgy, and especially their eagerness in embracing Christianity all show.

The success of the Utopians in leading the good life without the help of revelation is the basis of More's social satire. As Professor Chambers has said, "the underlying thought of *Utopia* always is, *with nothing save Reason to guide them, the Utopians do*

*this: and yet we Christian Englishmen, we Christian Europeans
. . . !"* The happiness of the Utopians is an eloquent commentary
on the discrepancy between the Western World as it is (whether
in the sixteenth or twentieth centuries) and what it might be, if
we could curb pride and pursue the life of reason.

Like their communism, the religious toleration of the Utopians
is less "modern" than it seems at first glance. Since they have only
reason as their guide, they cannot know the true God with cer-
tainty. A few of them identify God with the sun or a planet or
some very good man of bygone days. Most of them believe
in a single all-powerful and unknowable God who is not identi-
fiable with anything in the Creation. They are *all* monotheists,
and they all believe in the immortality of the soul. Within these
limits, reason permits some variety of belief (a variety denied to
Europeans by their knowledge of the Gospels). The limits of
toleration are rigidly enforced. A Utopian may deny the immortality of the soul, but he must keep his opinion to himself. If he
tries to persuade others to his belief, More clearly implies, he is
liable to bondage, and, for a continued offense, to death.

Utopia has a special interest for the light it throws on its author's life. King Henry VIII induced men of great abilities to
serve him. Most of them did so willingly enough, sharing the am-
bitions and motives of their master. More accepted office under
Henry, and was used as an unwilling tool to achieve the very
aims he opposed. How could he reconcile his employment to his
conscience? To put the question in broader terms, how can a
good man serve a wicked king? The issue is discussed in Book I
of *Utopia,* and we may be sure that More took office in the hope
that if he could not pursue good policies, he could at least mitigate bad ones. He was quite aware of the latent conflict between
the King's will and his own principles. He realized the probable
outcome of the conflict, and tried to prepare his family long in
advance. King Henry liked More and knew him well. He was
quite aware of More's firmness, and probably understood More's
attitude in taking office. As Book I of Utopia shows, their relationship was ironic, potentially tragic, from the time More first
accepted office. With every step upward on the ladder of court

advancement, and with every failure in deterring the King from war and conquest, the irony and the suspense were heightened. More's very foresight was a kind of dramatic foreshadowing. When the foreseen break came, More faced death with the magnanimity of a tragic hero and the constancy of a martyr. Henry could kill but not corrupt him. In killing More, Henry added greatly to the cogency of Hythloday's argument in Book I against serving kings. Was More's decision to serve a king wrong, his career a mistake, his death folly?

Translator's Note

The first translation into English of More's *Utopia* was by
Ralph Robinson, published in 1551. The second was by Bishop
Gilbert Burnet, published in 1685. Both are excellent translations
and both have been reprinted many times. Neither is altogether
accurate and neither is easily read by the modern student. The
present translation is an entirely new one, but both Robinson's
and Burnet's translations (especially the latter) have been consulted throughout, and their wording has sometimes been followed or adapted. Eight of the section headings in Book II have
been added; the others are in the original Latin. No other changes
from the original have been made.

Principal Dates in More's Life

1478 Birth February 6.

1485 *Henry VII ascends the throne.*

c.1490-2 More in the household of Lord Chancellor Morton.

c.1492-4 At Oxford.

1494-6 More a law student at New Inn, then at Lincoln's Inn.

1497 Made a barrister at Lincoln's Inn.

1500 Erasmus and More become intimate friends.

c.1501 Studies Greek with Lily, Grocyn, and Linacre.

1504 Elected to Parliament.

1505 Marries Jane Colt.

1507 *Americus Vespucius'* Four Voyages *published in Latin.*

1509 *Accession of Henry VIII at the age of seventeen.*
      Erasmus writes The Praise of Folly *in More's house in London.*

1510 More appointed Under-Sheriff of London.

1511 His wife dies and he marries Mistress Alice Middleton.

1515 More goes to Flanders as one of the King's ambassadors.
      Book II of *Utopia* written. *Wolsey made Lord Chancellor.*

1516 Book I of *Utopia* written, and the book is published in November at Louvain.

1518 More accepts office on the King's Council.

1521 Made Under-Treasurer.

1529 Succeeds Wolsey as Lord Chancellor.

1531 *Thomas Cromwell appointed to the King's Council.*

1532 More resigns the Lord Chancellorship.

1533 *Anne Boleyn crowned Queen.*

1534 On April 17 More refuses to take an oath accepting the King as Supreme Head of the Church, and is imprisoned in the Tower.

1535 More is tried, convicted on perjured evidence, and beheaded on July 6.

UTOPIA

Book I

The most victorious and trimphant King of England, Henry the Eighth of that name, in all royal virtues a prince most peerless, had recently some differences with Charles, the most serene Prince of Castile, and sent me into Flanders to negotiate and compose matters between them. I was colleague and companion to that incomparable man, Cuthbert Tunstall, whom the king lately made Master of the Rolls to the great satisfaction of all. I will say nothing of this man, not because I fear the testimony of a friend will be questioned, but because his learning and virtues are greater than I can describe. And also they are so well-known that they do not need my commendation, unless I would, according to the proverb, "Show the sun with a lantern."

The men appointed by the prince to treat with us, all excellent men, met us at Bruges according to agreement. The chief man among them and their leader was the Margrave of Bruges, a distinguished man. But the wisest and best spoken was George Temse, the Provost of Cassel, a man eloquent both by nature and training, very learned in the law, and most skillful in affairs through his capacity and long practice. After we had met several times and could not come to an agreement, they went to Brussels for some days to learn their prince's pleasure.

Meanwhile I went to Antwerp, since our business permitted it. Of those who visited me while I was there, Peter Giles was more congenial to me than any of the others. He was a native of Antwerp, a man much respected there and worthy of the highest regard. I do not know of a more cultivated or a better bred young man anywhere. He is, indeed, the best and most learned of men, and besides, very courteous to all. To his intimates he is so loving, so trustworthy, and so deeply affectionate that it would be very hard to find another friend like him anywhere. No man is more modest or more candid. No man unites more simplicity

with prudence. His conversation is so pleasant, and so witty without vulgarity, that the fervent desire I felt to see my native country
and my wife and children (from whom I had been away more
than four months) was much eased by his company.

One day after I had heard mass at Nôtre Dame, the most
beautiful and most frequented church in Antwerp, I was about
to return to my lodgings when I happened to see him talking
with a stranger, a man well advanced in years. The stranger had
a sunburned face, a long beard, and a cloak hanging carelessly
from his shoulders. From his appearance and clothing I took him
to be a seaman. When Peter saw me, he approached and greeted
me. As I was returning his salutation, he took me aside, and
pointing to the stranger, said, "Do you see that man? I was just
thinking of bringing him to you."

"He would have been very welcome on your account," I answered.

"And on his own, too," he said, "if you knew him, for there
is no man alive who can tell you so much about unknown peoples and countries. And I know that you are most eager for such
information."

"Then," said I, "I did not guess badly, for at first sight I took
him for a seaman."

"No," he replied, "you are mistaken, for he has sailed not as
the sailor Palinurus, but as Ulysses, or rather as Plato.[1] This
Raphael, surnamed Hythloday [2] (for so he is called), though not
ignorant of the Latin tongue, is eminently learned in the Greek.
He has applied himself more particularly to Greek because he has
given himself wholly to philosophy, in which he knew that the
Romans have left us nothing that is valuable except what is to be
found in Seneca and Cicero. He was so desirous of seeing the
world that he divided his patrimony among his brothers (he is
Portuguese by birth), and threw in his lot with Americus Vespucius. He took part in the last three of Vespucius's four voyages,
accounts of which are now published. But he did not return home
with him on the last voyage. After much effort, he won permission from Americus to be one of the twenty-four who were left in
a fort at the farthest place at which they touched in their last

1. Palinurus was Aeneas' pilot. As a sailor he is here contrasted to Ulysses, who was regarded during the Renaissance as a profound student of men,
manners and government, and to Plato.
2. From the Greek *huthlos,* nonsense.

voyage. Being left thus was highly gratifying to a man who gave more thought to his travels than to his burial place, and who often used to say that one who has no grave is covered by the sky and that the road to heaven is equally short from all places.

"Yet this disposition of mind would have cost him dear if God had not been very gracious to him. After the departure of Vespucius he travelled over many countries with five companions from the fort. At last by singular good fortune he got to Ceylon and from thence to Calcutta, where he very happily found some Portuguese ships. And so, beyond anyone's expectation, he came back to his own country."

When Peter had told me this, I thanked him for his kindness in wishing to make me acquainted with a man whose conversation he knew would be so acceptable to me, and I turned toward Raphael. Upon that Raphael and I greeted one another. And after the ordinary civilities of strangers upon their first meeting, we all went to my house. There in the garden we sat down on a grassy bank and conversed.

He told us that when Vespucius had sailed away, he and his companions that had stayed behind in the fort often met the people of the country, and by fair and gentle speech gradually won their favor. Before long they came to dwell with them quite safely and even familiarly. He also told us that they were esteemed by the prince (I have forgotten his name and his country), who furnished them plentifully with all things necessary, and who also gave them the means of traveling, both boats when they went by water and wagons when they traveled over land. He sent with them a faithful guide who was to introduce and recommend them to such other princes as they had a mind to see. After many days' journey, they came to towns and cities, and to commonwealths that were both well peopled and happily governed.

Under the equator and as far on both sides of it as the sun moves, there lie vast deserts parched with the perpetual heat of the sun. The whole region is desolate and gloomy, savage and uncultivated, inhabited by wild beasts and serpents, and by a few men as wild and dangerous as the beasts themselves. As they went on, conditions gradually grew milder. The heat was less burning, the earth greener, and even the beasts less fierce. At last they found nations, cities, and towns that had mutual commerce among themselves and with their neighbors, and that traded by sea and land with remote countries. From then on, he said, they were able to visit many lands on all sides, for they were welcome on board any ship about to make a voyage.

The first vessels that they saw were flat-bottomed, with sails made of close-woven reeds and wicker, or in some places of leather. Farther on they found ships made with round keels and canvas sails, in all ways like our ships. The seamen were skillful both in sailing and in navigation. They were most grateful to him, Raphael said, for showing them the use of the compass, of which they had been ignorant. For that reason they had sailed with great caution and only in summer. Now they have such confidence in the compass that they no longer fear winter, and are carefree rather than safe. This discovery, which they thought so much to their advantage, may become the cause of much mischief to them through their imprudence.

It would take too long to set forth all that Raphael told us he had observed, and it would be a digression from our present purpose. Perhaps in another place we shall tell more about the things that are worth knowing, especially about the wise and prudent institutions that he observed among the civilized nations. We asked him many questions about such things and he answered us very willingly. We made no inquiries, however, about monsters, which are common enough. Scyllas, ravenous harpies, and cannibals are easy to find anywhere, but it is not so easy to find states that are well and wisely governed.

While he told us of many things which are amiss among those new-found nations, he also reckoned up not a few things from which patterns might be taken for correcting the errors of our own cities and kingdoms. These I shall treat in another place, as I have said. Now I intend to relate only what he told us about the manners and laws of the Utopians, first setting forth the occasion that led us to speak of that commonwealth. Raphael had been talking very wisely about the numerous errors and also the wise institutions found both among those nations and us, speaking as intimately about the customs and government of each place he had visited as though he had lived there all his life. Peter was struck with admiration.

"I wonder, Master Raphael," he said, "why you do not enter some king's service, for I know of no prince who would not be eager to have you. Your learning and your knowledge of places and men would entertain him pleasantly, while your advice and

your examples would be invaluable. Thus you would serve your
own interest and be useful to all your friends."

"I am not greatly concerned about my friends," he said, "for I
have already done my duty toward them. While I was still young
and healthy, I distributed among my relations and friends the
possessions which other men do not part with till they are old and
sick (and then only grudgingly and because they can no longer
keep them). I think my friends should rest content with this and
not expect that for their sake I should enslave myself to any king
whatsoever."

"Well-said," Peter replied, "but I do not mean that you should
be a slave to any king, only that you should be of service to him."

"The difference is a mere matter of words," Raphael replied.

"As you will," said Peter, "but I do not see any other way in
which you can be so useful either to your friends or to the public,
to say nothing of making yourself happier."

"Happier?" exclaimed Raphael. "Would a way of life so ab-
horrent to my nature make my life happier? Now I live as I will,
and I believe very few courtiers can say that. As a matter of fact,
there are so many men courting the favor of the great that it will
be no great loss if they have to do without me or others like me."

Then I said, "It is clear, Master Raphael, that you desire
neither wealth nor power, and indeed I value and admire such a
man much more than I do any of the great men in the world.
Yet I think, if you would give your time and effort to public affairs, you would do a thing worthy of a generous and philosophi-
cal nature like yours, even though you might not enjoy it. You
could best perform such a service by belonging to the council of
some great prince, whom you would urge on to whatever is noble
and just. I know you would do this, if you were in such a post.
And your efforts would be effective, because a people's welfare or
misery flows wholly from their prince, as from a never-failing
spring. Your learning is so full, even when not combined with
experience, and your experience so great, even without learning,
that you would be an exceptional couneillor to any king whatsoever."

"You are doubly mistaken, my dear More," said he, "both in
your opinion of me and in your estimate of the situation itself. I
do not have that capacity which you fancy to be in me, and if I
had it, the public would not be any better off through the sacrifice
of my leisure; for most princes apply themselves to warlike pur-

suits (in which I have no skill or interest) rather than to the useful arts of peace. They are generally more set on acquiring new kingdoms rightly or wrongly, than on governing well those that they already have. Moreover the councillors of kings are so wise that they need no advice from others (or at least so it seems to themselves). At the same time they accept and even applaud the most absurd statements of men whose favor they seek for the sake of standing well with the prince. It is natural that each man should flatter himself by thinking his own opinions best. The old crow loves his young and the ape his cubs. Now in a court made up of those who envy all others and admire only themselves, if a man should propose something that he had read in history or observed in his travels, the other councillors would fear that their whole reputation for wisdom was in danger, and that they would be regarded as plain fools unless they could show his suggestion was weak and defective. If all else failed, they would take refuge in the retort that such and such things pleased our ancestors and would that we could match their wisdom! With this they would settle down as though they had said the last word on the subject and as though there were a terrible danger in finding a man wiser than our ancestors in anything. We readily follow whatever they did, as though it were necessarily best. But if something better is proposed, we seize the excuse of reverence for past times and cling to it doggedly. I have met with these proud, absurd, and morose judgments in many places, and once even in England."

"Were you ever in England?" I asked.

"Yes, I was," he answered, "and stayed there some months, not long after the uprising of the Cornishmen against the King had been suppressed with great slaughter of the poor people engaged in it.[3] I was then under great obligation to the reverend prelate, John Morton,[4] Archbishop of Canterbury, Cardinal, and at that time Chancellor of England, a man, my dear Peter (and Master More knows I speak the truth) as much respected for his wisdom and virtue as for his great authority. He was of middle height, not bent with age. His looks aroused respect rather than fear. His conversation was easy, but serious and grave. Sometimes he liked to test the spirit and presence of mind of the suitors who came to him on business by speaking sharply though not discourteously

3. In 1497. Some 2000 rebels were slain.
4. Born c. 1420, died 1500. As a boy of twelve and thirteen, More lived two years in his household, and was then sent to Oxford by him.

to them. He liked to discover these qualities, which were characteristic of his own nature, as long as they were not carried to the point of impudence, and he thought men who had them were best fitted for administering affairs. He was eminently skilled in the law, and had vast understanding and a prodigious memory. He had improved his extraordinary natural abilities by study and experience. When I was in England, the King depended greatly on his advice, and the government seemed to be chiefly supported by him. He left school for the court when little more than a boy, and devoted all his life to state affairs. Having endured many changes of fortune, he had acquired at great cost a vast stock of wisdom, which is not soon lost when purchased so dear.

"One day when I was dining with him, there was present an English counselor-at-law, who took occasion to praise at some length the severe execution of justice upon theives, who, as he said, at that time were being hanged so fast that there were sometimes twenty on one gibbet. Then he exclaimed that he could not understand how there could be so many thieves everywhere, when so few escaped hanging. Upon this I made bold to speak freely before the Cardinal, and said, 'There is no reason to wonder at the matter. This way of punishing thieves is neither just in itself nor good for the public. The remedy is not effectual, because the severity is too great. Simple theft is not so great a crime that it ought to cost a man his life, and no punishment however severe is sufficient to restrain a man from robbery who can find no other livelihood. In this not only you in England but a great part of the world seem to imitate bad masters, who are readier to punish their pupils than to teach them. Severe and horrible punishments are enacted against theft, when it would be much better to enable every man to earn his livelihood, instead of being driven to the fatal necessity of stealing and then dying for it.'

"'Care enough has been taken for that,' said the counselor. 'There are handicrafts and there is farming by which men may make a living, unless they choose to pursue evil.'

"'That won't do,' I said. 'We may overlook the maimed men who return home from foreign and civil wars, as lately from the Cornish Uprising and, before that, from your war with France. These men, mutilated in the service of king and country, can no longer follow their old trades, and are too old to learn new ones. But since wars occur only intermittently, let us overlook these men, and consider those things that happen every day. There are a great many noblemen who live idly like drones, and subsist on the labor of their tenants, whom they bleed white by rack-renting (this being the only instance of their frugality, for they are prodigal in every thing else even to the extent of beggaring themselves). These noblemen carry around with them a great train of idle fellows, who have never learned any trade by which they can earn a living. As soon as their lord dies or they themselves fall ill, they are straightway turned out of doors, for lords would rather support idlers than sick men, and often the heir is unable to support so great a household as his father did. Those who are turned off soon take to starving, unless they take to stealing. What else can they do? When they have worn out their health and their clothes, and their faces look starved and their garments are tattered, men of quality will not deign to take them on. And country people dare not do so, for they know that one who has been bred up in idleness and pleasure and has been used to walking about with sword and buckler looks down on the whole neighborhood and despises everybody as beneath him. Such a man is not fit for spade and mattock, and will not serve a poor man faithfully for a small wage and a sparse diet.'

" 'These men ought to be particularly cherished among us,' said the lawyer. 'In case of war the strength of our army depends on them, because they have a bolder and nobler spirit than workmen and farmers have.'

" 'You may as well say that we should encourage thieves on account of wars,' I answered, 'for you will never lack thieves so long as you have the others. Just as thieves sometimes turn out to brave soldiers, soldiers often prove to be very industrious robbers, so closely are these two ways of life related. The custom of keeping too many retainers is widespread here, but it is not peculiar to this nation. It is common to almost all people. In France there is an even more troublesome kind of men, for the whole country is full of soldiers who are maintained in time of peace—if such a state of affairs can be called peace. They are kept on pay for the same reason that you have given for your noblemen's keeping their idle retainers. Wise fools have a maxim that it is necessary for the public safety always to have in readiness a strong army, preferably of veteran soldiers. They think inexperienced men are not to be depended on, and they sometimes even seek occasions for making war, in order that they may have trained soldiers and ready cutthroats, or as Sallust puts it, that hand and spirit may

not grow dull through idleness. But France has learned to her
cost how dangerous it is to feed such beasts. The fate of the Romans, the Carthaginians, the Syrians, and many other peoples
shows the same thing, for their government, their fields, and even
their cities were ruined by their own standing armies. How un-
necessary this preparedness is appears from the fact that the
French soldiers trained in arms from their youth cannot boast of
having often got the better of your raw men. Lest I seem to flatter
you now, I shall not say more on this point. But neither your
town workmen nor your farm laborers are thought to be much
afraid of figthing the idle followers of gentlemen, provided they
are not disabled by some accident or weakened by extreme want.
So you need not fear that the strong vigorous men (it is only such
men that noblemen will keep around them), who grow soft and
flabby from their lazy and effeminate life, would be weakened if
they were taught useful crafts by which to earn their living and if
they were disciplined to manly labor. Anyway, it seems most un-
reasonable that you should maintain a host of men in anticipation
of war, when you never have war unless you wish it and when
you will always be disturbed by so many idle men in peace, which
is always to be more considered than war. However, I do not
think that the compulsion to steal arises from this alone. There is
another cause that is more peculiar to England.'

" 'What is that?' the Cardinal inquired.

" 'Your sheep,' I replied, 'that used to be so gentle and eat so
little. Now they are becoming so greedy and so fierce that they
devour the men themselves, so to speak. They lay waste and pil-
lage fields, homes, and towns. For wherever the sheep yield a
softer and richer wool than ordinary, there the nobility and gentlemen, yea even the holy men and abbots, are not content with
the old rents which their lands yielded. They are no longer satisfied to live in idleness and luxury without benefiting society.
They must needs injure the commonwealth. They leave no land
for cultivation, they enclose all the land for pastures, they destroy
houses and demolish towns, keeping only the churches, and these
for sheep barns. As though forests and game preserves were not
already taking up too much land, these worthy men turn all
dwelling places and fields into a dessert. So one convetous insatiable glutton, a veritable plague to his native country, may enclose
many thousand acres of land together within one hedge. The tenants are turned out, and by trickery or main force, or by being

worn out through ill usage, are compelled to sell their possessions. These miserable people, men, women, husbands, wives, orphans, widows, parents with little children, whole families, poor but numerous (since farming requires many hands), are forced to move out. They leave their familiar hearths and can find no place where they may settle down. They sell their household goods, which would not bring much even if they could wait for a buyer, for little or nothing. When that little money is gone (and it will soon be spent), what is left for them to do but steal and so be hanged, doubtless justly, or to go about begging? And if they beg, they are thrown into prison as idle vagabonds. They would willingly work, but can find no one who will hire them. There is no need for farm labor, to which they have been bred, when there is no arable land left. One herdsman can look after a flock of sheep large enough to stock an area that would require many hands if it were ploughed and reaped.

" 'This enclosure has likewise raised the price of grain in many places. The price of wool has also risen so much that poor people who used to make cloth are no longer able to buy it, and this makes many more idle. For since the increase of pasture the sheep rot has killed off a vast number of them, as though God had sent down a plague to punish the avarice of the owners, upon whom it might more justly have fallen than upon the sheep. But even if the number of sheep should increase greatly, their price is not likely to fall. Though they cannot be called a monopoly, because they are not engrossed by one person, yet they are in so few hands and these so rich that, as the owners are not pressed to sell them sooner than they have a mind to, they never sell until they have raised the price as high as possible.

" 'For the same reason the price of other kinds of livestock is just as high, and this all the more because with so many villages being pulled down and all country tasks being greatly neglected, there are not enough people to look after the breeding of cattle. The rich do not breed cattle as they do sheep, but buy them lean at a low price, and after fattening them on their own pastures, sell them at a high price. I do not think that the bad effects of this are all felt as yet. Up to this time there is a scarcity only in those places where the fattened cattle are sold. But when in time rich men buy up the cattle faster than they can be bred, then there will be a decreasing supply where men do their buying, and ultimately a widespread shortage. So your island, which seemed especially fortunate in this respect, is endangered by the base avarice of a few.

"'Moreover the high price of grain causes rich men to dismiss as many retainers as possible from their households. What, I ask, can those who are dismissed do but either rob or beg? And a man of high spirit is more likely to rob than to beg.

"'To make this wretched poverty worse, wanton luxury is yoked to it. In noblemen's households, and even among tradesmen and farmers and all ranks of people, there is costly vanity in clothing and wasteful extravagance in eating. Look at the eating houses, the bawdy houses of one kind or another, the taverns and alehouses. And look at the many games like dice, cards, football, tennis, and quoits, in which money slips away so fast. Do not all these pursuits lead their followers straight to robbery? Banish these plagues, make those who have ruined farms and villages restore them or rent them to landlords who will. Curb the engrossing of land by the rich, which amounts almost to monopoly. Let fewer be supported in idleness. Let agriculture be restored and wool manufacture be revived, so there will be productive work for the useless throng who have become thieves through want or idleness.

"'If you do not find a remedy for these evils, it is idle to boast of your severity in punishing theft. Your policy may have the appearance of justice, but it is really neither just nor expedient. If you allow people to be badly brought up and their habits to be corrupted little by little from childhood, and if you then punish them for crimes to which their early training has disposed them, what else is this, I ask, but first making them thieves and then punishing them for it?'

"While I was speaking thus, the counselor had made ready to answer and had chosen the formal manner of disputants who are more diligent in summing up than in replying, apparently regarding the memory as worthy of chief praise. So he said to me, 'You have talked very well for a stranger, but you have heard of more things than you have been able to gain exact knowledge about. I will make the matter clear to you directly. First I will repeat in order what you have said. Then I will show you how you have been mislead by your ignorance of our affairs. And, finally, I will refute all your arguments. First, I will begin where I promised. Four things you seemed to me'—

"'Hold your peace,' said the Cardinal, 'for you will not finish soon when you begin thus. We will relieve you of the trouble of answering now, and postpone your reply until our next meeting, which shall be tomorrow if Raphael's affairs and yours will permit it. But now, Master Raphael, I would gladly know why you think theft ought not to be punished by death, and why you would decree some other punishment which would be more expedient for the public welfare. For certainly you would not leave theft unpunished. And since death itself does not restrain men, what force or fear could restrain evildoers, if they thought their lives would be safe? On the contrary, they would look on the mitigation of the punishment as an invitation to commit more crimes.'

" 'It seems to me, most kind father,' I said, 'a very unjust thing to take away a man's life for a little money, for nothing in the world can be of equal value with a man's life. If they say that it is not for the money that one suffers but for the violation of justice and the transgression of laws, then may not extreme justice be called extreme injury? For we ought not to approve of these terrible laws that draw the sword for the smallest offenses. Nor ought we approve of the Stoic view that considers all crimes as equal, as if there were no difference between killing a man and snatching his purse. If we judge impartially, there is no likeness nor relationship between them. God has forbidden us to kill; shall we kill so readily for the theft of a little money? But if it is argued that killing is forbidden by God's law except in so far as human law declares that a man ought to be killed, what prevents men from making other laws in the same way, even to the extent of making prostitution, adultery, and perjury lawful? God has taken from each person the right of killing another, and even of killing himself. If it is pretended that mutual consent to human laws on manslaughter can free those who kill from the divine law, what is this but preferring human law to the law of God? Doubtless the result will be that men will determine how far all the laws of God should be observed. Although the Mosaic law is harsh and severe, as if for an enslaved and stubborn people, it punishes theft with a fine, not death. Let us not think that in his new law of mercy, wherein he treats us with the tenderness of a father, God has given us a greater license to cruelty than he did to the Jews. These are the reasons why I think it is wrong to put thieves to death. Anybody knows how absurd and even dangerous to the public welfare it is to punish a thief and a murderer equally. If a thief sees no less danger threatens him if condemned for theft than for murder, he will kill the person whom otherwise he would only have robbed. When the punishment is the same, there is more security in murder and a greater expectation of concealing the crime by killing the witness. So while we strive to terrify thieves with excessive cruelty, we really incite them to kill innocent men.

"'Now as to the question of what better punishment can be found, in my judgment it is much easier to find a better one than a worse. Why should we doubt the value of the kind of punishment long used by the Romans, who were most skillful in the arts of government? They condemned those convicted of great crimes to work in stone quarries and to dig in mines with chains upon them for life. But in the matter of punishment I prefer the method which I observed in my travels in Persia among those commonly called the Polylerites.[5] They are a considerable and well-governed people, subject only to their own laws except that they pay annual tribute to the Persian king. They live far from the sea and are nearly surrounded by mountains. Being contented with the products of their own country, which is fruitful, they have little trade with any other nation. According to their traditional policy they do not strive to enlarge their boundaries, so that their mountains and the tribute which they pay to their overlords secure them from all invasions. Thus they have no wars. They live in a comfortable rather than a splendid manner, and may be called happy rather than distinguished or famous. Indeed I doubt if they are known even by name to any but their immediate neighbors. Whoever among them is found guilty of theft must make restitution to the owner, and not (as elsewhere) to the prince. They hold that the prince has no more right to the stolen goods than the thief. If the stolen property no longer exists, the value of the thief's property is estimated and restitution is made from it. The entire remainder is assigned to the thief's wife and children.

"'Those convicted of theft are sentenced to serve in public works, but are neither imprisoned nor chained, unless their crimes were heinous. If they shirk and do their tasks lazily, they are whipped. If they work hard, they are treated without any mark of reproach, except that at night after roll call they are locked up in their sleeping rooms. Aside from their constant

5. From the Greek *polus leros*, much nonsense.

labor, they suffer no discomfort in living. As they work for the
state, they are well fed out of the public stores. The cost of main-
taining them is handled differently in different parts of the country. In some places they are supported by alms. Uncertain though
this support may seem, the Polylerites are so benevolent that no
way is found more satisfactory. In some places public revenues are
set aside, or a poll tax is levied for their support. In other places
they are not set to public work, but anyone in need of workmen
goes to the market place and hires them by the day at a fixed rate,
a little lower than that for free men. If they are lazy, it is lawful to
whip them. In this way there is never a lack of work for them,
and every one of them brings something into the public treasury
beyond his living.

" 'They are all dressed in the same color. Their hair is not
shaved off, but cut short about the ears, and a little of one ear is
cut off. Their friends are allowed to give either food, drink, or
clothing (as long as it is of the proper color). But to give them
money is death, both to the giver and to the recipient. Nor is it a
less serious offense for any free man to take money from them for
any reason whatsoever. It is also a capital crime for any of these
bondmen, as they are called, to handle weapons. In each district
of the country they are distinguished by a special mark. It is a
capital offense to get rid of the mark, or to go out of their own
district, or to talk with a slave of another district. Attempted
escape is as punishable as escape itself. It is death for any other
slave to be accessory to escape, and servitude for any free man.
On the other hand there are rewards for informers: money for a
free man, liberty for a slave, and for both of them pardon and
forgiveness, in order that it may never be safer for them to persist
in a plan of escape than to repent of it.

" 'Such are their laws and policy in this matter. You can easily
see how mild and advantageous they are, for the aim of the
punishment is only to destroy vice and so to save men. The
wrongdoers are so treated that they see the necessity of being
honest, and for the rest of their lives they make up for the wrong
they have done. There is so little danger of their falling back into
their old ways that travelers going from one part of the country
to another consider them more trustworthy than other guides,
changing them at the boundary of each district. For the bondmen
have no means of committing robbery; they are unarmed, and
any money in their possession is an evidence of crime. If caught,

they would be punished at once, and there is no hope of escape anywhere. Since each piece of a bondman's clothing is unlike the customary clothing of the country, how could a bondman escape unless he fled naked? And even then his cropped ear would betray him as a fugitive. Might not the bondmen form a conspiracy against the government? That indeed is a danger. But how could the bondmen of any one district enter into a plot without a general conspiracy among the bondmen of the other districts? Such a conspiracy cannot be formed, since they are not allowed to meet or talk together. No one would risk a plot, when secrecy is so dangerous and betrayal so advantageous to the informer. Besides, none of them are quite hopeless of recovering freedom, since they may expect to be freed finally if they are obedient and patient and give promise of future good conduct. Every year some are pardoned as a reward for their patience.'

"When I had related all this, I added that I saw no reason why this method could not also be followed in England, and with much greater advantage than the 'justice' which the counselor had praised so highly.

"To this the counselor replied that such a system could never be set up in England without endangering the whole nation. As he said this, he shook his head, made a wry face, and then held his peace. All the company seemed to be of his opinion.

"'It is hard,' the Cardinal said, 'to foresee whether it would work well or not, since no trial has yet been made of it. But when the death sentence has been passed upon a thief, the King might reprieve him for a while without right of sanctuary, and so test how the plan worked. If it proved advantageous, then he might establish it. If not, he would execute punishment upon the man formerly condemned. This would be no more disadvantageous or unjust than if the condemned man had been put to death earlier, and there would be no risk involved. I think vagabonds, too, should be treated in this way. We have passed many laws against them, but have produced no effect as yet.'

"When the Cardinal had said this, they all fell to praising the ideas which they had scorned when suggested by me. And they praised particularly the idea about vagabonds, because it had been added by the Cardinal.

"I do not know whether it is worthwhile to tell what followed, as it was ridiculous, but I shall tell it, for it is not a bad story and it is relevant to our subject in a way. There was a hanger-on standing around who played the fool so naturally that he seemed to be one. His jokes were so cold and dull that we laughed more at him than at them. Yet sometimes he said something witty, bearing out the old proverb that he who throws the dice often will sometimes make a lucky throw. One of the company had just said that I had taken care of the thieves and the Cardinal had taken care of the vagabonds, so that nothing remained but to make public provision for the poor whom sickness or old age had disabled.

" 'Leave that to me,' said the fool, 'and I shall see that it is done properly. There is no sort of person I had rather have out of my sight, having been so often vexed with them and their sad complaints. No matter how lugubriously they beg for money, they never whine so well as to get a single penny from me. Either I have no mind to give them anything, or when I have a mind to it, I have nothing to give them. Now they know me so well that they don't waste their breath on me, but let me pass without giving me any trouble, hoping for nothing from me. No more, by Hercules, than if I were a priest. But I would have a law passed sending all these beggars to monasteries, the men to the Benedictines to become lay brothers, as they call them, and the women to be nuns.'

"The Cardinal smiled and passed it off as a joke. The rest liked it in earnest. But a certain friar, learned in divinity, took such pleasure in this jest on priests and monks that, although he was ordinarily a grave man almost to the point of severity, he began to jest. 'You will not free yourself from beggars,' he retorted, 'unless you take care of us friars too.'

" 'You have been taken care of already,' answered the fool. 'The Cardinal has provided for you handsomely in his proposals for restraining vagabonds and setting them to work, because you friars are the greatest vagabonds of all.'

"When the company with their eyes on the Cardinal saw that he was not ill pleased with this jest, they began to enjoy it, all except the friar. He, as you may easily imagine, was touched to the quick, and so incensed that he could not refrain from railing at the fool. He called him knave, backbiter, slanderer, sent him to the devil, and uttered dreadful threats out of Holy Scripture.

"Then the jester began to jest in earnest, as he was clearly on his own ground. 'Be not angry, good friar,' he said, 'for it is written, "In patience possess your soul." '

"In reply the friar said, and I shall quote his own words, 'I am not angry, you rogue, or at least I do not sin in it. For the psalmist says, "Be ye angry and sin not." '

"Then the Cardinal gently cautioned him to calm himself. 'No, my lord,' he replied, 'I speak only from great zeal, as I ought to do. For holy men have great zeal. As it is said, "The zeal of thy house hath eaten me up," and we sing in church, "those who mocked Elisha for being bald, as he went up to the house of God, felt the effects of his zeal." [6] Just so that villain, that rogue, that ribald jester shall feel it.'

" 'You do this, perhaps, with good intention,' said the Cardinal, 'but you would act in a more holy way, or certainly more wisely, if you would not set your wit against a fool's wit and engage in an argument with a jester.'

" 'No, my lord,' the friar answered, 'I would not act more wisely. For Solomon, the wisest of men said, "Answer a fool according to his folly." That is what I am doing now. I am showing the pit into which he will fall unless he takes heed. For if the many mockers of Elisha, who was only one bald man, felt the effect of his zeal, how much more effect shall one mocker of many friars feel among whom are so many bald men? And besides, we also have a papal bull by which all who mock us are excommunicated.'

"When the Cardinal saw that there was no end of this matter, he made a sign to the fool to leave and turned the conversation to another subject. Soon after, he rose from the table, and dismissing us, went to hear petitioners.

"With what a long story, Master More, I have burdened you. I would be ashamed to have done so if you had not earnestly requested it; you seemed to listen as though you did not wish to miss any of it. I might have shortened my account somewhat, but I have told it in full so that you might see how those who scorned what I proposed approved of it as soon as they saw that the Cardinal did not dislike it. In fact they went so far in their flattery that they applauded in good earnest things that he approved only as a fool's jest. From this account you can see how little courtiers would value me or my advice."

To this I answered, "you have done me a great kindness, my dear Raphael, in speaking so wisely and at the same time so pleasantly. As you spoke, I seemed to be a child and in my own

6. See 2 Kings 11: 23.

country once more, through the pleasant recollection of that cardinal in whose family I was raised in my boyhood. Dear as you
are to me on other accounts, you cannot imagine, Master Raphael,
how much dearer you are because you honor his memory so
highly. Nevertheless I cannot yet change my opinion. I still think
that if you could overcome the aversion you have to the courts of
princes, you might do a great deal of good to mankind by the
advice that you would give. And this is the chief duty of every
good man. Your Plato thinks that commonwealths will only become happy when either philosophers become kings or kings
become philosophers.[7] No wonder we are so far from happiness
when philosophers do not deign to assist kings with their coun-
sels."

"They are not so inhuman but that they would willingly do
it," Raphael replied. "In fact they have already done it in many
books which have been published, if only those in power would
read their good advice. Doubtless Plato judged right that unless
kings became philosophers, they would never abide by the coun-
sels of philosophers, imbued as they are and infected with false
values from boyhood up. Plato himself found this to be true of
Dionysius of Syracuse. If I were at the court of some king and
proposed wise laws to him and tried to root out of him the dangerous seeds of evil, do you not think I would either be thrown
out of his court or held in scorn?

"Imagine me at the court of the King of France. Suppose I
were sitting in his council with the King himself presiding, and
that the wisest men were earnestly discussing by what methods
and intrigues the King might keep Milan, recover Naples so
often lost, then overthrow the Venetians and subdue all Italy, and
add Flanders, Brabant, and even all Burgundy to his realm, besides some other nations he had planned to invade. One man
urges him to make an alliance with the Venetians (to last as long
as expedient), to share plans with them, and even give them
some of the spoils, which can be got back when things work out
according to plan. One proposes hiring German mercenaries and
paying the Swiss to be neutral. Another suggests propitiating His
Imperial Majesty with gold, as with a holy sacrifice. Still others
think that peace should be made with the King of Aragon, and
Navarre restored to him to cement the peace. Another man
thinks that the Prince of Castile ought to be ensnared with the

7. *Republic,* 473d.

hope of an alliance, and some of his courtiers won over to the French interest with pensions. The hardest problem of all is what to do with England. A treaty of peace must be negotiated with them, as strong as possible, since a weak alliance must be bound by the strongest possible bonds. They must be called friends, but suspected as enemies, and the Scots must be kept in readiness to attack them, in case they stir ever so little. Also a banished noble-man who has pretensions to the English crown must be secretly supported (treaties prevent its being done openly), as a means of bringing pressure to bear on the English King and holding him to the treaty.

"Now in this great ferment, with so many brilliant men plan-ning together how to carry on war, imagine so modest a man as myself standing up and urging them to change all their plans, to leave Italy alone and stay at home, since the kingdom of France is indeed greater than one man can govern well, so that he ought not to think of adding others to it. Then imagine that I should tell them about the great decree of the Achorians,[8] who live near the island of Utopia to the southeast. Long ago these people engaged in a war to gain another kingdom for their king, who inherited an ancient claim to it through marriage. When they had conquered it, they found that keeping it was as hard as getting it. Their new subjects were always rebelling or being invaded by foreign aggressors, so that the Achorians were always at war either for them or against them, and thus could never disband their army. In the meantime taxes lay heavy on them, money went out of their kingdom and their blood was sacrificed to their king's glory, though their peace was none the more secure. Their morals were corrupted by war. Their thirst for plunder and violence became confirmed. Their laws were falling into contempt, because their king, distracted with the cares of the two kingdoms, was unable to give adequate care to either. When they saw that there would be no end of these evils, they agreed to make a humble address to their king, desiring him to choose which of the kingdoms he had the greatest mind to keep, since he could not hold them both. They were too numer-ous a people, they said, to be governed by half a king. A man would not even share his mule-driver with another. So this good prince was constrained to be content with his old kingdom, and give his new one to a friend (who was not long after driven out).

8. From the Greek *a-choros,* no place.

"Finally imagine that I told the French King's council that these wars would throw whole nations into social chaos, would exhaust the King's treasury and destroy his own people, and yet in the end through some mischance might all be fought for nothing. I would urge the King to tend his ancestral kingdom and improve it as much as he could. He should love his people and be loved by them. He should live among them and govern them gently, and let other kingdoms alone, since his own is big enough, if not too big for him. Pray how do you think such a speech as this would be taken?"

"I admit, not very well," I said.

"Then let us proceed," he said. "Suppose the councillors are discussing how they can raise money for the King's treasury. One man recommends increasing the value of money when the King pays his debts and decreasing it when he collects his revenues. Another proposes a pretence of war that money may be raised to carry it on; then when the money is in, making peace, so that the people will attribute the peace to the piety of their prince and to his tender care for the lives of his subjects. A third calls to mind some old moth-eaten laws, regarded as antiquated by long disuse, forgotten by the King's subjects and consequently broken. He proposes levying the penalties for breaking these laws, so that the King will get a great sum of money as well as credit for executing the law and doing justice. A fourth proposes forbidding many things under severe penalties, especially such as are contrary to the public interest, and then dispensing with these prohibitions for money. By this means the King pleases his people and makes a double profit. He can impose heavy fines on transgressors, and the more he gets for selling licenses, the more solicitous he seems about his people's welfare, since he will do nothing contrary to the public interest except for a huge price. Another proposes that the judges be coerced to decide all cases in favor of the King. They should be summoned to court often, so that the King may hear them argue cases in which he is concerned. However unjust his claims may be, one or another of the judges, from love of contradiction or from pride in singularity or in order to win favor with the King, will find some opening or other to twist the law in his favor. If the judges can be brought to differ in opinion, the clearest thing in the world is made disputable and the truth is brought into question. Then the King has the opportunity of interpreting the law to his own advantage. The judges that hold out will be won over to the King's side either through fear or diffidence. Then they may be expected to give judgment boldly in the King's favor. There are always convenient pretexts for giving judgments favorable to the King. It will be said that equity lies on his side, or that the words of the law are in his favor, or that their meaning is intricate and obscure; or finally, what will always outweigh any law with dutiful judges, an appeal will be made to the King's undoubted prerogative.

"Thus all the councillors agree with the maxims of Crassus: a king can never have enough money, since he has to maintain his army; a king can do nothing unjustly even if he wants to; all property belongs to the king, even the very persons of his subjects; no man has any other property than what the king out of his goodness thinks fit to leave him; the king should leave him as little as possible, as if it were to his advantage that his people should have neither riches nor liberty. For wealth and freedom make men less submissive to a cruel and unjust rule, whereas poverty dulls them, makes them patient, and bears down and breaks that spirit which might otherwise dispose them to rebel.

"Now what if after this advice was given, I should get up and assert that such counsel was both dishonorable and ruinous to a king? And that both his honor and his safety consisted more in his people's wealth than in his own. Suppose I should maintain that men choose a king not for his sake, but for theirs, that by his care and efforts they may live comfortably and safely. And that therefore a prince ought to take more care of his people's happiness than of his own, as a shepherd ought to take more care of his flock than of himself. Certainly it is wrong to think that the poverty of the people is a safeguard of public peace. Who quarrel more than beggars do? Who long for a change more earnestly than the dissatisfied? Or who rushes in to create disorders which such desperate boldness as the man who has nothing to lose and everything to gain? If a king is so hated and scorned by his subjects that he can rule them only by insults, ill-usage, confiscation, and impoverishment, it would certainly be better for him to quit his kingdom than to keep the name of authority when he has lost the majesty of kingship through his misrule. It is less befitting the dignity of a king to reign over beggars than over rich and happy subjects. Thus Fabricius, a man of noble and exalted spirit, said he would rather govern rich men than be rich himself. When a ruler enjoys wealth and

pleasure while all about him are grieving and groaning, he acts
as a jailor rather than as a king. He is a poor physician who cannot cure a disease except by throwing his patient into another.
A king who can only rule his people by taking from them the
pleasures of life shows that he does not know how to govern
free men. He ought to shake off either his sloth or his pride, for
the people's hatred and scorn arise from these faults in him. Let
him live on his own income without wronging others, and limit
his expenses to his revenue. Let him curb crime, and by his wise
conduct prevent it rather than allow it to increase, only to punish
it subsequently. Let him not rashly revive laws already abrogated
by disuse, especially if they have been long forgotten and never
wanted. And let him never seize any property on the ground
that it is forfeited as a fine, when a judge would regard a subject
as wicked and fraudulent for claiming it.

"But suppose I should go on to tell the King's council of the
law of the Macarians,[9] a people who live not far from Utopia.
On the day that their king begins to reign, he must take an oath
confirmed by solemn ceremonies never to have more than a
thousand pounds of gold in his treasury, or the equivalent to
that in silver. They say that an excellent king, who cared more
for the prosperity of his country than for his own wealth, made
this law as a barrier against heaping up so much treasure as to
impoverish his people. He thought that sum would suffice,
whether the ruler had occasion to use it against rebels or to protect the kingdom against the invasion of an enemy, but would
not be enough to encourage the ruler to invade foreign countries.
This last was his chief purpose in making the law. He also
thought that by this provision there would not be a shortage of
money for use in daily business. And when a king must distribute
among the people whatever comes into his treasury above the
legal amount, he will not be disposed to oppress his subjects.
Such a king as this will be a terror to evil-doers and will be loved
by all good men. If I should press these views on men strongly
inclined to the contrary, how deaf they would be to it all!"

"Stone deaf, no doubt," I said, "and no wonder! To tell the
truth, it seems to me that you should not offer advice which you
know will not be considered. What good could it do? How could
such a bold discourse influence men whose minds are prepossessed
and deeply imbued with contrary aims? Such academic phi-

9. From the Greek *makarios*, blessed.

iosophy is not unpleasant among friends in free conversation, but in the King's council, where official business is being carried on, there is no room for it."

"That is what I was saying," Raphael replied. "There is no place for philosophy in the councils of princes."

"Yes, there is," I said, "but not for the speculative philosophy which thinks all things suitable for all occasions. There is another philosophy that is more urbane, that takes its proper cue and fits itself to the drama being played, acting its part aptly and well. This is the philosophy you should use. When one of Plautus's comedies is being played and the slaves are joking together, what if you should suddenly appear on the stage in a philosopher's garb and repeat Seneca's speech to Nero from the *Octavia*? Would it not be better to say nothing than to make a silly tragicomedy by mixing opposites? You ruin a play when you add irrelevant and jarring speeches, even if they are better than the play. So go through with the drama in hand as best you can, and do not spoil it because another more pleasing comes into your mind.

"So it is in a commonwealth and in the councils of princes. If evil opinions cannot be quite rooted out, and if you cannot correct habitual attitudes as you wish, you must not therefore abandon the commonwealth. Don't give up the ship in a storm, because you cannot control the winds. And do not force unheard-of advice upon people, when you know that their minds are different from yours. You must strive to guide policy indirectly, so that you make the best of things, and what you cannot turn to good, you can at least make less bad. For it is impossible to do all things well unless all men are good, and this I do not expect to see for a long time."

"The only result of this," he answered, "will be that while I try to cure others of madness, I myself will rave along with them. If I am to speak the truth, these are the things I must say. Whether a philosopher can speak falsely, I do not know, but certainly I can't. Though my advice may be exasperating to them, I do not know why it should seem presumptuous to the point of absurdity. If I should advocate policies such as Plato describes in his *Republic* or as the Utopians actually practice in their country, policies which are certainly much better than those I have urged, they would, I admit, be out of place. For in those commonwealths all things are held in common, while here property is owned privately. But what have I urged that might not or should not be said anywhere? Of course my discourse cannot please those who rush headlong the opposite way; it checks them and shows them their dangers.

"If we ignore as crude and absurd everything that the evil customs of men have made unusual, then even among Christians we shall have to ignore most of Christ's commandments, though He bade us not to whisper them, but to proclaim them from the house-tops. Most of his precepts disagree with our way of living far more than my discourse does. But preachers, who are indeed clever men, seem to have followed your counsel. Seeing that men will not fit their ways to Christ's pattern, the preachers have fitted His teaching (as though it were a leaden rule) to human customs, to get agreement somehow or other. The only result I can see is that men become more confirmed in their wickedness.

"And this is all I could achieve in a prince's court. For either I would think different thoughts from the rest, and that would be as if I had no thoughts, or else I would agree with them and thus (as Terence's Mitio says) [10] be an accessory to their madness. I do not understand what you mean by saying that a man should guide policy indirectly and should strive to make the best of things, so that what is bad will at least be made as good as possible. In councils there is no place for silent and unwilling acquiescence. A man must openly approve of the worst plans and consent to the most pernicious resolutions. One would pass for a spy or even a traitor, if he approved of such plans only grudgingly. A man has no chance to do good when his colleagues are more likely to corrupt the best of men than be corrected themselves. He will either be corrupted himself by his colleagues, or, if he remains sound and innocent, he will be blamed for the folly and knavery of others. He is far from being able to mend matters by guiding policy indirectly!

"That is why Plato in an excellent simile showed that wise men will not meddle in affairs of state.[11] They see the people swarm into the streets and get drenched with rain, and they cannot persuade them to go out of the rain and back to their houses. They know that if they should go out to them, they would accomplish nothing, and be drenched themselves. So they stay indoors. Although they cannot remedy the folly of others, they can at least be wise themselves.

10. *Adelphi*, I, ii, 66.   11. *Republic*, 496d.

"But, Master More, to speak plainly what is in my mind, as long as there is private property and while money is the standard of all things, I do not think that a nation can be governed either justly or happily: not justly, because the best things will fall to the worst men; nor happily, because all things will be divided among a few. Even these few are not really well off, while the rest are utterly miserable.

"So I reflect on the wise and sacred institutions of the Utopians, who are so well governed with so few laws. Among them virtue has its due reward, yet everything is shared equally and every man lives in plenty. I contrast them with other nations that are still making laws and yet can never order their affairs satisfactorily. Although each man calls the property he has obtained his own, the many laws passed every day do not enable him to obtain or keep it or to distinguish satisfactorily what he calls his own from another's. This is clear from the many lawsuits unceasingly arising and never ending. When I consider these things, I grow more favorable to Plato's opinion and do not wonder that he refused to make laws for any people who will not share all their goods equally. Wisest of men, he easily perceived that the one and only way to make a people happy is to establish equality of property.[12] I doubt whether this equality can be achieved where property belongs to individual men. For when every man gets as much as he can for himself by one device or another, the few divide the whole wealth among themselves and leave want to the rest. The result generally is that there will be two sorts of people, and their fortunes ought to be interchanged: one sort are useless, but ravenous and wicked, while the other sort are unassuming, modest men who serve the public more than themselves by their daily work.

"By this I am persuaded that unless private property is entirely done away with, there can be no fair distribution of goods, nor can the world be happily governed. As long as private property remains, the largest and far the best part of mankind will be oppressed with an inescapable load of cares and anxieties. This load, I admit, may be lightened somewhat, but cannot be entirely removed. Laws might be made that no one should own more than a certain amount of land nor possess more than a certain sum of money. Or laws might be passed to prevent the prince

12. A reference to an incident in the life of Plato related by Diogenes Laertius.

from growing too powerful and the populace from becoming too strong. It might be made unlawful for public offices to be solicited, or sold, or made burdensome for the officeholder by great expense. Otherwise officeholders are tempted to reimburse themselves by dishonesty and force, and it becomes necessary to find rich men for those offices which ought rather to be held by wise men. Such laws, I say, may have as much effect as good nursing has on men who are dangerously sick. Social evils may be allayed and mitigated, but so long as private property remains, there is no hope at all that they may be healed and society restored to good health. While you try to cure one part, you aggravate the disease in other parts. In redressing one evil another is committed, since you cannot give something to one man without taking the same thing from another."

"On the contrary," I replied, "it seems to me that men cannot live well where all things are in common. How can there be plenty where every man stops working? The hope of gain will not drive him; he will rely on others and become lazy. If men are stirred by want, and yet no one can legally protect what he has earned, what can follow but continual bloodshed and turmoil, especially when the respect for and the authority of magistrates are lost? I cannot conceive of authority among men that are equal to one another in all things."

"I do not wonder," said Raphael, "that it appears so to you, since you have no idea, or only a false idea of such a state. But if you had been with me in Utopia and had seen their customs and institutions as I did at first hand for the five years that I spent among them, you would frankly confess that you had never seen a people ordered so well as they were. Indeed I would never willingly have left, if it had not been to make known that new world to others."

"You will not easily persuade me," Peter Giles said, "that people in that new land are better governed than in our known world. Our abilities are not inferior to theirs, and our government, I believe, is older. Long experience has helped us to find out many conveniences of life, and by good luck we have discovered other things which man's abilities could never have invented."

"As for the age of their commonwealth," Raphael replied, "you might judge more correctly if you had read their histories. If these may be trusted, they had cities even before there were inhabitants here. What chance has hit on or ingenuity has discovered, these things might have been found there as well as here. As a matter of fact I believe that we surpass them in natural abilities, but we are left far behind them in diligence and in zeal to learn. According to their chronicles they had heard nothing about the men from beyond the equator (as they call us) before our landing there, except that once about twelve hundred years ago a ship which a storm had carried toward Utopia was wrecked on their island. Some Romans and Egyptians from the ship were cast up on the island and never departed. Now note how the Utopians profited from this chance event by their diligence. They learned all the useful arts of Roman civilization either directly from their shipwrecked guests or indirectly from hints given in answer to inquiries. What benefits from the mere fact that some Europeans landed there! If a similar accident has hitherto brought any men here from their land, it has been completely forgotten, as doubtless it will be forgotten in time to come that I was ever in their country. From one such accident they made themselves masters of all our useful inventions, but I believe it will be a long time before we accept any of their institutions which are better than ours. This willingness to learn, I think, is the real reason for their being better governed and for their living more happily than we do, though we are not behind them in ingenuity or riches."

"Then I earnestly beg you, Master Raphael," I said, "to describe that island to us. Do not try to be brief, but explain in order everything relating to their soil, rivers, towns, people, manners, institutions, laws, and, in fact, everything you think we would like to know. And you may take it for granted that we want to know whatever we do not know yet."

"There is nothing," he said, "that I would be happier to do, for these things are fresh in my mind. But it will take some time."

"Let us first go to dinner," I said, "and afterward we shall have time enough."

"Let us do so," he said. So we went in and had dinner. Then we came back and sat down on the same bench. I ordered my servants to take care that no one should interrupt us. Peter Giles and I besought Raphael to be as good as his word. When he saw that we were eager to hear him, he sat silent and thoughtful a moment, and then began as follows. . . .

Book II

THEIR COUNTRY AND AGRICULTURE

The island of Utopia is two hundred miles in breadth in the middle part where it is widest, and it is nowhere much narrower than this except toward the two ends. These ends, drawn around in a five hundred-mile curve, make the island crescent-shaped. Between the horns of the crescent, which are some eleven miles apart, the sea comes in and spreads into a great bay. Being well secured from the wind, the bay does not rage with great waves, but is quiet like a lake. This makes nearly the whole inner coast a harbor, greatly facilitating mutual trade. But the entrance into the bay, what with shallows on one side and rocks on the other, is very dangerous. Near the middle there is one rock that rises above the water, and so is not dangerous. On the top of it a tower has been built, in which a garrison is kept. The other rocks lie under water and are very treacherous. The channels are known only to the Utopians, so if any stranger should chance to enter the bay without one of their pilots, he would run a great danger of shipwreck. Even they themselves could not enter safely if some marks on the coast did not direct their way. If these were shifted even a little, any fleet coming against them, no matter how great it was, would certainly be lost.

On the other side of the island there are likewise many harbors, and the coast is so fortified by nature and art that a small number of men could hold off the attack of a great force. They say (and the appearance of the place bears this out) that their land was once not an island. But Utopus, who conquered the country and gave it his name (it was previously called Abraxa), brought its rude and uncivilized inhabitants to such a high level of culture and humanity that now they excel all other people in that part of the world. When he had subdued them, he cut a channel fifteen miles long where their land joined the continent and thus brought the sea entirely around their land. He not only forced the natives to work at it, but his soldiers too, so that the natives would not think they were treated like slaves. By putting so many men to work, he finished the project quickly, and the neighbors, who at first had laughed at his folly, were struck with admiration and terror at his success.

There are fifty-four cities on the island, all large and well built, and with the same language, customs, institutions, and laws. All of them are built on the same plan, as far as the location permits. The nearest are at least twenty-four miles apart, and those that are farthest are not so far but that a man can go on foot from one city to the next in a day.

Once a year each city sends three of its wisest elders to Amaurot [13] to consult about their common concerns. Amaurot is the chief city of the island and lies near its center, so that it is the most convenient place for the elders to meet. Every city has enough ground assigned to it so that it has at least ten miles of farm land in every direction. Where the cities are farther apart, they have more ground. No city desires to enlarge its bounds, for the inhabitants consider themselves husbandmen rather than landlords. They have built houses all over the countryside, well designed and furnished with farm equipment. These houses are inhabited by citizens who come to the country by turns to dwell in them. No country household has fewer than forty men and women in it, besides two bondmen. A master and mistress, serious and mature persons, are in charge of each household. A magistrate is placed over every thirty households. Every year twenty from each household move back to the city, after completing a two-year turn in the country. In their place twenty others are sent out from town, to learn farm work from those that have already been in the country for a year and are somewhat skilled in it. In turn they must teach those who come the following year. If they were all equally ignorant of farm work and new to it, they might damage the crops through ignorance. This custom of shifting the farm workers is established in order that no one will have to do this hard work against his will for more than two years, but many of them ask to stay longer because they take a natural delight in farm life.

The farm workers till the soil, care for the cattle, hew wood, and take it to the city by land or water, as is most convenient. They breed an enormous number of chickens by a marvelous method. Men hatch the eggs, not hens, by keeping them in a

13. From the Greek *amauros*, dim, uncertain.

warm place at an even temperature. The chicks, as soon as they come out of the shell, recognize and follow men instead of their mothers.

They raise very few horses, but these are full of mettle and are kept only for exercising the youth in the art of horsemanship. For the work of plowing and hauling they employ only oxen. They think horses are stronger than oxen, but they find that oxen can hold out longer and are less subject to disease, and so can be kept with less cost and effort. Moreover, when they are too old for work, they can be used for meat.

They raise grain only for bread. They drink wine, apple or pear cider, or water, sometimes clear, but often mixed with honey or liquorish, of which they have an abundance. Although they know just how much grain each city and its district will consume, they sow more grain and breed more cattle than they need for their own use, and share the surplus with their neighbors. When they need goods on the farms which they do not make there, they get them from the town magistrates without giving anything in exchange. This is not inconvenient, since most of them go to town once a month, especially on holidays. When harvest time comes, the country magistrates notify the towns how many hands will be needed. The harvesters come at the right time, and commonly get in the whole harvest in one fair day.

THEIR CITIES AND ESPECIALLY AMAUROT

If you know one of their cities, you know them all, so like are they to one another, except where the location makes some difference. So I shall describe one of them, and no matter which. But what one rather than Amaurot, whose eminence the other cities acknowledge in sending their elders to the annual meeting there, and which I know best because I lived there five years?

Amaurot lies on a gently sloping hill, and is almost square in shape. From a little below the top of the hill it runs down two miles to the river Anyder,[14] and it follows along the river bank for a somewhat greater distance. The Anyder rises about eighty miles above Amaurot in a small spring, but other streams flow into it, two of them being of some size, so that, as it runs past Amaurot, it has grown to the width of half a mile. It grows

14. From the Greek *an-hudor,* without water.

larger and larger, until at last sixty miles farther along it is lost in the ocean. In this stretch of river between the city and the sea, and also for some miles above the city, the water ebbs and flows every six hours with a strong current. When the tide comes in, it fills the whole Anyder with salt water for about thirty miles, and forces back the fresh water. Above this for several miles the water is brackish, but a little higher up, as it runs past the city, it is quite fresh. When the tide ebbs, the water is fresh all the way to the sea. Over the river there is a bridge, not built on wooden piles, but on many stately arches of stone. It is placed at the part of the city farthest from the sea, so that ships can sail along the entire side of the city without being stopped. They have also another stream, not large to be sure, but very gentle and pleasing. It rises out of the hill, and after flowing through the town in a steep descent, joins the Anyder. The inhabitants have fortified the fountainhead of this river, which rises a little outside the town, so that if they should be attacked, the enemy would not be able to cut off or divert the stream or poison it. Water from it is carried in pipes into the lower section of town. Where the water of the small river cannot be conveyed, they collect rain water in cisterns.

The town is surrounded by a high thick wall with many towers and forts. Also running around the city on three sides, there is a dry ditch, broad and deep and thick-set with a thorn hedge. The river is on the fourth side. The streets are conveniently laid out both for vehicles and for protection from the wind. Their buildings are by no means unsightly, with unbroken rows of houses facing each other and running along the streets through the whole town. The streets are twenty feet wide. Through the whole length of the city there are large gardens behind the houses and enclosed by them.

Every house has a door to the street and another to the garden. The doors, which are made with two leaves, open easily and swing shut of their own accord, freely letting anyone in (for there is no private property). Every ten years they change houses by lot. They think much of their gardens. They raise vines, fruits, herbs, and flowers, all so tastefully arrayed and so well kept that I have never seen any gardens more fruitful or more beautiful than theirs. Their interest in gardening is kept up both by the pleasure they find in it and also by the rivalry between the inhabitants of the different streets, who vie with each other in this matter. Indeed you will find nothing else in this whole city more useful to the citizens or more pleasant. It seems that the founder of the city arranged for nothing more carefully than the gardens.

They say that the whole city was planned by King Utopus himself, but that he left to posterity matters of ornamentation and improvement which could not be perfected in one man's lifetime. Their records go back 1760 years to the conquest of the island and are preserved with the greatest care. From these it appears that at first their houses were small, like cottages and peasant huts, built out of any sort of timber with mud walls and thatched roofs. Now their houses are three stories high; their fronts are faced with stone, cement, or brick, with rubble thrown in between the facings of the walls. The roofs are flat, and are covered with a kind of plaster that is cheap and fireproof and that resists weather better than lead. They use glass very frequently in their windows to keep out the wind. They also use thin linen cloth treated with oil or gum so that it lets in the light and keeps out the wind better.

THEIR MAGISTRATES

Each year thirty households choose a magistrate, formerly called the syphogrant, but now called the phylarch.[15] Over each ten syphogrants and the households subject to them there is another magistrate, once called the tranibor but now called the chief phylarch. All the syphogrants, two hundred in number, choose the prince by secret vote from the list of four men whom the people of the four sections of the city have nominated. The syphogrants are under oath to choose the man they think fittest. The prince is chosen for life, unless he is suspected of trying to become a dictator. They choose the tranibors annually, but they rarely change them. All their other magistrates hold office for only a year.

The tranibors meet every third day, and more often if necessary, to consult with the prince on affairs of state or on the few disputes between private persons. The tranibors always call in two syphogrants to the senate, different ones every day. It is a

15. *Phylarch* is a Greek word meaning chief of a tribe or clan. No satisfactory derivation of syphogrant and tranibor is known.

rule that no decision on public business can be made unless the matter has been considered on three different days in the senate. It is a capital offense to consult together on public affairs outside the senate or the people's assembly.

These provisions have been made so that the prince and the tranibors may not conspire together to change the government and enslave the people. Matters of great importance are first brought to the assembly of the syphogrants. When they have discussed the matter with their households and have themselves consulted together, the syphogrants report their decision to the senate. Sometimes an issue is referred to the council of the whole island. One practice observed in their senate is never to debate a matter on the same day on which it was first introduced. Instead, they defer the question to the next meeting, so that a man will not let his tongue run away with him and then strive to defend his foolish first-thoughts instead of considering the public good. They know that through a perverse and preposterous pride a man may prefer to sacrifice the common good to his own hasty opinions for fear of being thought heedless and shortsighted. To prevent this, they take care to deliberate wisely rather than speedily.

THEIR ECONOMY AND OCCUPATIONS

All the Utopians, men and women alike, work at agriculture, and no one is inexperienced in it. They are trained in it from childhood, partly by school instruction and partly by practice. School children are often taken into the nearby fields as though for play, where they not only see men and women working, but get exercise by working themselves.

Besides sharing in the farm work, every person has some particular trade of his own, such as the manufacture of wool or linen, masonry, metal work, or carpentry. There is no other craft which is practiced by any considerable number of them. People wear the same sort of clothes throughout the island, except for the distinctions which mark the difference between the married and the unmarried. The fashion of clothing never changes. Their clothing looks well, does not hinder their movements, and is suitable both for summer and winter. Every household makes its own clothing, but each man and woman also learns one of the other trades I have mentioned. The women, being the weaker, practice the lighter crafts, such as working with wool or linen. The heavier crafts are left to the men. Generally the same trade passes down from father to son, often by natural inclination. But if anyone's interests lies elsewhere, he is adopted into a family practicing the trade he prefers. When anyone makes such a change, both his father and the magistrates see to it that he is transferred to a responsible and upright householder. After a man has learned one trade, if he desires to acquire another, it is managed in the same manner. When he has learned both, he follows whichever he likes better, unless the public has special need for the other.

The chief and almost the only business of the syphogrants is to see that no one sits around in idleness, and that everyone works hard at his trade. But no one has to wear himself out with endless toil from morning till night, as if he were a beast of burden. Such a life, though it is the common life of workmen in all other countries, is no better than a slave's. The Utopians work six hours out of the twenty-four. They work three hours before dinner. After dinner they rest two hours, and then go to work for another three hours. Then they have supper and at eight o'clock, counting from noon, they go to bed and sleep eight hours.

The other hours of the day, those that are not used for work, sleep, and meals, are left to their individual choice, on the understanding that they shall not waste them idly and wantonly. They use their free time busily on any pursuit that pleases them. Many of them fill these intervals with reading. They have the custom of giving public lectures daily before daybreak, which none are obliged to attend except such as are selected for the pursuit of learning. Yet a great many from all ranks, both men and women, go to hear lectures of one sort or another, according to their interests. If anyone whose mind does not delight in intellectual pursuits prefers to spend his free time at his trade, as many do, this is not forbidden, but commended as beneficial to the commonwealth. After supper they spend an hour in some recreation, in summer gardening, in winter diverting themselves in their dining halls with music or talk. They know nothing about gambling with dice or other such foolish and ruinous games. They play two games not unlike our chess. One is a battle of numbers, in which one number plunders another. The other is a game in which the vices battle against the virtues. In this game the co-operation of the vices against the virtues and their opposition to each other is shown up very cleverly, as well as the special oppositions between particular virtues and vices, and the methods by which the vices openly assault or secretly undermine the virtues, and how the virtues break the strength of the vices and by what means finally one side or the other wins the victory.

To understand their way of life fully we must look at one point more carefully. They allot only six hours to labor, and you might think that a scarcity of essential goods would result. Actually their working hours are sufficient to provide not only an abundance, but even a superabundance of all the necessities and conveniences of life. You will easily understand this if you consider how large a part of the population in other countries is idle. In the first place, the women (and they are half the whole population) usually do not work, or if they do, their husbands lie snoring. Secondly, there is the multitude of priests and so-called religious men, as numerous as they are idle. Add to these all the rich men, especially great landlords, who are commonly called well-born and noble. Add their henchmen, the whole flock of swaggering bullies. Reckon in with these the strong and lusty beggars, who go about feigning some disease to excuse their laziness. You will find that the actual number of workers who supply the needs of mankind is much smaller than you would think. And now consider how few of these workers are employed in really necessary work. Because we measure values by money, we have to carry on many superfluous trades to support luxury and wantoness. If the multitude of our workers produced only what men need for good living, there would be such an abundance of goods that prices would go down and workmen could not subsist. You can easily imagine how little time would be enough to produce the goods that man's needs and convenience demand (and his pleasure too if it were true and natural pleasure), if only the workers in useless trades were placed in worthwhile occupations and all the idlers who languish in sloth but eat twice as much as laborers were put to work on useful tasks.

The truth of this supposition is very apparent in Utopia. Out of all the men and women whose age or health permit them to work, scarcely five hundred are exempted in each city and its surrounding area. Among these are the syphogrants, who are excused from labor by law. Yet they do not excuse themselves from it, because they incite others to work more easily by setting them an example. The Utopians grant the same exemption to some who apply themselves exclusively to learning, but only at the recommendation of the priests and in accordance with a secret vote of the syphogrants. If one of these persons disappoints their hopes, he is made a workman again. On the other hand it sometimes happens that a worker devotes his free time so zealously to learning and progresses so far through his diligence, that he is excused from his trade and is transferred to the class of the learned men. From this class are chosen ambassadors, priests, tranibors, and the prince himself (of old called the Barzanes, but later the Ademus).[16] Since the rest of the entire population is neither idle nor engaged in useless occupations, it is easy to understand how they produce so much in so short a work day.

Besides all this, it should be noted that they accomplish more with less work than people do elsewhere. Among other people the building and repair of houses requires the continuous labor of many workmen. Often a thriftless heir lets the house which his father built fall into disrepair, and his successor must repair at great cost what he might have kept up at small charge. It also happens oftentimes that a house built at a vast expense is scorned and neglected by an heir of supposedly finer taste, and when in a short time it falls into ruin, he builds another somewhere else at no less expense. But among the Utopians things are so ordered that they seldom choose a new location for building a house. They are quick to make present repairs and careful to preserve their buildings for a very long time with a minimum of labor. In the interims craftsmen in the building trades have hardly anything to do, unless they hew timber and square stones for future building.

Consider how little labor their clothing requires. For work they wear loose-fitting leather clothes, which last as long as seven years. When they go out, they put on a cloak which covers up their rougher clothing. Throughout the entire island their cloaks are the same color, the natural color of wool. They need less cloth than is used elsewhere and what they do need is much less costly. They use linen cloth most, because it takes less work to make. They like linen cloth to be white and woolen cloth to be

16. Ademus is from the Greek *a-demos*, without a people. Barzanes has not been explained.

clean, but they are indifferent to fineness of texture. Each person is generally satisfied with one cloak every two years, whereas in other countries four or five woolen coats of different colors and the same number of silk cloaks will scarcely suffice for one man, and for more fastidious men even ten are not enough. Among the Utopians there is no reason why a person should want more clothes. If he had them, he would not be any better protected against the cold, nor would he seem at all better dressed.

When they have accumulated a great abundance of everything as a result of their moderate consumption and of their all working, great numbers of them go out to work on the roads, if any need repairing. Often when there is no need for public work, the magistrates proclaim a shorter workday, since they never employ the citizens on needless labor. For the chief aim of their institutions and government, above all else, is to give all citizens as much time as public needs permit for freeing and developing their minds. In this they suppose the felicity of man's life to consist.

THEIR SOCIAL AND BUSINESS RELATIONS

Now I must explain the social arrangements of these people, their dealings with each other, and how they distribute their goods among themselves.

Each community consists of households for the most part made up of kinsfolk. When the women grow up and are married, they move to their husbands' homes. The sons and grandsons remain in the household and obey their oldest common parent, unless his mind has begun to fail with age. In that case the next oldest takes his place. In order that their cities may not have too many or too few inhabitants, they allow no city to have over six thousand households (exclusive of the surrounding country district) and no household to have fewer than ten or more than sixteen adults. The number of children is not restricted, but the number is easily controlled by transferring the children of a household that has too many to one that does not have enough. Likewise if any city has too many people, that city makes good any shortage in the other cities.

If there is too great an increase throughout the entire island, they take a certain number of citizens from the different cities and plant a colony on the adjoining mainland, where the in-habitants still have more land than they can well cultivate. If the natives wish to live with the Utopians, they are taken in. Since they join the colony willingly, they quickly adopt the same institutions and customs. This is advantageous for both peoples. For by their policies and practices the Utopians make the land yield an abundance for all, which before seemed too small and barren for the natives alone. If the natives will not conform to their laws, they drive them out of the area they claim for them-selves, waging war if they meet resistance. Indeed they account it a very just cause of war if a people possess land that they leave idle and uncultivated and refuse the use and occupancy of it to others who according to the law of nature ought to be supported from it.

If the population of any of their cities happens to decline so much that it cannot be made good from other parts of the island without reducing the size of the other cities too much, then the population is built up with citizens from the colonies. This has happened only twice in all their history, both times the result of a devastating plague. They prefer their colonies to die off rather than allow any of their island cities to grow too small.

To return to their manner of living together: as I said, the eldest of every household governs it. Wives are subject to their husbands, children to their parents, and the younger to their elders. Every city is divided into four equal parts, and in the middle of each quarter is a market place for all kinds of goods. The products of each household are brought here and stored in warehouses, where each kind of goods is kept in its proper place. Here the head of each household looks for what he needs, and takes what he wants without payment or obligation. Why should anything be refused him? There is enough of everything, and no fear that anyone will claim more than he needs. Why should anyone be suspected of asking for more than is necessary, when there is never any shortage? Men and animals alike are greedy and rapacious from fear of want. Only human pride glories in surpassing others in conspicuous consumption. For this kind of vice there is no room whatsoever in the Utopian way of life.

Adjoining the warehouses there are food markets where all sorts of vegetables, fruit, and bread are brought. Fish, meat, and poultry are also brought there from places outside the city near running water, where bondmen do the slaughtering and cleaning. The citizens are not allowed to do the slaughtering. The Utopians think that slaughtering destroys the sense of compassion, the most distinctively human feeling of our nature. They do not allow anything dirty or filthy to be brought into the city, to keep the air from becoming tainted with the stench and as a result infectious.

Every street has its great public halls, equally distant from each other and each known by its own name. The syphogrants live in these. Fifteen of the thirty households of a syphogrant live on one side of the hall, fifteen on the other. Here the thirty households are assigned to eat their meals. The stewards of each hall go to the market place at a certain time to secure food.

In distributing food, the Utopians' first concern is for the sick, who are cared for in public hospitals. Every city has four hospitals, generally built outside the walls and so roomy that they might pass for little towns. No matter how great the number of sick people, they need not be crowded closely or uncomfortably. And if the sick have some contagious disease, they can be isolated. These hospitals are well arranged and well supplied with everything needed to cure the patients, who are nursed with watchful and tender care. They are constantly attended by most skillful physicians. Consequently no one objects to being sent to the hospital, everyone preferring to be sick there than at home.

When the steward of the sick has received the food prescribed by the doctors, the rest is divided fairly among the halls in proportion to their numbers, except that they have due respect for the prince, the chief priest, and the tranibors, and also ambassadors and all strangers, if there are any. The few strangers who come there, and they come but seldom, are entertained in certain well-furnished houses.

At the hours of lunch and dinner at the sound of a bronze trumpet, the whole syphogranty assembles in its hall, except for those sick abed in the hospital or at home. It is not forbidden for anyone to take food home from the market place after supplies have been taken to the hall. They know that nobody would do this except for some good reason. While it is not forbidden to eat at home, it is not thought proper. Besides no one would be so foolish as to prepare a poor meal at home when there is a sumptuous one ready for him so near at hand.

In the syphogrants' halls bondmen do the dirtiest and heaviest work. The women of each family take turns in preparing and cooking the food and in serving the whole meal.

They sit at three tables or more, according to their number. The men sit on the wall side and the women opposite, so that if a woman feels sick suddenly (as sometimes happens in pregnancy), she may get up without disturbing the others, and go to the room where the nurses sit with the nursing infants. Here there are always cradles and clean water and a fire, so that they may lay the infants down, change them, dress them before the fire, and play with them.

Each child is nursed by its own mother, unless death or illness prevents. In that case the syphogrant's wife quickly finds a nurse. This is not hard to do. Any woman who can gladly offers herself for this duty, and all the Utopians applaud her kindness. Also the child regards its nurse as its mother.

All the children under five years of age sit together in the nurses' room. The rest of the children too young for marriage, both boys and girls, either wait on the tables, or if not old enough for that, stand near by in complete silence. They eat whatever is handed to them by those sitting at table, and no other time is set for their meals.

In the upper part of the dining hall, the syphogrant and his wife sit at the center of the first table. This is considered the place of honor, and from this table, which is placed crosswise, the whole company can be seen. Two of the oldest sit next to them, for they always sit four to a group. If a church is situated in that syphogranty, then the priest and his wife preside with the syphogrant and his wife. On each side are seated first younger and then older people. In this way throughout the hall those of about the same age sit together, yet they are mingled with others not of their age. This was planned, they say, so that the dignity of the elders and the respect due them might restrain the youth from indecent words and gestures, for nothing done or said at table can escape the notice of those near by on either side.

The best of each kind of food is first served to the elders, whose places are distinguished by some mark. Then the rest are served all alike. The elders divide the choice bits, of which there is not enough to go around, as they wish. Thus due respect is paid them, yet all the rest fare as well as they do.

They begin every lunch and dinner with reading something on good manners and morals, but this is brief, so as not to be distasteful. Then the elders engage in conversation, which must not be either stern or dull. The elders do not talk throughout the meal, but gladly listen to the younger men. In fact, they purposely lead them to talk, in order to discover their natural qualities in the freedom of mealtime conversation.

They eat a small meal at midday but a much larger evening meal, because lunch is followed by work, whereas dinner is followed by the night's rest, which they think aids good digestion. They never dine without music, and the second course always includes sweetmeats. They burn incense, scatter perfumes, and overlook nothing to make the diners merry. For they are inclined to believe that no kind of pleasure is forbidden, if it has no bad effects.

They live together in this manner in the city, but in the country, where they are farther separated from one another, they all eat at their own homes. And no country household is in want, for the provisions on which the city-dwellers live come from them.

THEIR TRAVELLING AND FOREIGN TRADE

If anyone wants to visit friends in another city or to see the country itself, he can easily get permission from his syphogrant and tranibor, unless he is needed for some particular work. Several travel together, taking a letter from the prince, which certifies that permission to travel has been granted and states the day of return. A wagon is furnished and a bondman to drive and look after the oxen; but unless women are in the company, they refuse the wagon as a needless trouble. They do not take anything with them, and they lack nothing on the whole journey. Wherever they are, they are at home. If they stay in one place longer than a day, each of them follows his own occupation and is welcomed by the artisans of the same craft.

If any man goes outside his district without leave and is caught without a passport from the prince, he is treated scornfully, brought back as a fugitive, and severely punished. If he does it again, he is made a bondman. Anyone who wants to walk through the fields of his own district, may do so with his father's permission and his wife's consent. Wherever he goes in the country, no food is given him until he has completed a forenoon's or an afternoon's work. On these terms he may go anywhere he wishes within the bounds of his district. For he would not be more useful to the community as a whole if he were inside the city.

So you see no loafing is tolerated, and there are no pretexts for laziness, or opportunities. There are no taverns or ale houses, no brothels, no chances for corruption, no hiding places, no secret meetings. Because they live in full view of all, they must do their accustomed labor and spend their leisure honorably. Such a manner of life must result in having plenty of everything, and since they all share it equally, it follows that no one can ever be in want or forced to beg.

In the annual senate at Amaurot (made up of three representatives from each city, as I have said), they find out what surpluses and shortages there are, and promptly assign the surplus of one place to supply the needs of another. This is done without charge; those who give receive nothing from those to whom they give. According to their plenty and scarcity, they supply or are supplied by each other, and so the whole island is, as it were, one household.

After they have provided enough for their whole island, and laid up enough for two years ahead because of the uncertainty of a single year's yield, they export the remainder to other countries, great quantities of grain, honey, wool, flax, wood, scarlet and purple dye stuff, hides, wax, tallow, leather, and also livestock. A seventh of everything they give to the poor of the country to which they export the goods, and the rest they sell at a moderate price. In exchange they import not only such goods as they lack at home (in fact, they lack little except iron), but also a great amount of silver and gold. They have carried on this trade a long time, and now have a greater supply of these metals than you would believe possible. So they care little now whether they sell for cash or credit, and for the most part accept promissory notes. In these they do not rely on the word of private individuals, but on the foreign city's official bond. When the day of payment comes, the foreign city collects the money due from the private debtors and returns it to its treasury, enjoying the profit until it is called in by the Utopians. Most of it is never called in. The Utopians think it unethical to take what is useless to them from those who can benefit by it. If they have reason to lend it to another people, they call it in.

Or they may need it for waging war. This is the only reason

for keeping at home all that treasure they have, as a protection to them in extreme peril or sudden danger. Since they would rather throw foreigners into battle than their own citizens, they use their treasure in war mainly for hiring mercenaries. They pay them exorbitant wages, in the hope of influencing the enemy. For they know that the enemy's soldiers can often be bought, or thrown into confusion by treason or even the suspicion of it.

THEIR GOLD AND SILVER, AND HOW THEY KEEP IT

Therefore they have accumulated an inestimable amount of gold and silver, but they do not keep it, in the form of treasure. I am reluctant to tell you how they keep it, for fear you will not believe me. I would not have believed it myself if anyone had told me about it—not unless I had seen it with my own eyes. It is almost always true that the more different anything is from what people are used to, the harder it is to believe. In view of the fact that the Utopians' customs are so different from ours, a shrewd judge will not be surprised to find that they do not use gold and silver at all as we do. Since they keep gold and silver only for grave contingencies, they take care that in the meantime no one shall value these metals more than they deserve. Iron is obviously greatly superior to either. Men can no more do without iron than without fire and water. But gold and silver have no indispensable qualities. Human folly has made them precious only because of their scarcity. Nature, like a wise and generous parent, has placed the best things everywhere and in the open, such as air and water and the earth itself, but she has hidden vain and useless things in remote and far away places.

If they kept their gold and silver guarded in a tower, foolish people might suspect the prince and senate of deceiving the citizens and aiming at some advantage for themselves. If they made plate and wrought-metal work out of them, they would not want to give up such articles and melt them down to pay mercenaries. To solve the problem, they have thought out a plan as much in accord with their institutions as it is contrary to ours. The plan seems incredible to us (except to those of us who are very wise), because we regard gold as of great value and hoard it carefully. While their eating and drinking utensils are made of china and glass, beautiful but inexpensive, their chamber pots and stools both in their public halls and their homes are made of gold and silver. They also use these metals for the chains and fetters of their bondmen. They hang gold rings from the ears of criminals, place gold rings on their fingers, gold collars around their necks, and gold crowns on their heads. Thus they hold gold and silver up to scorn in every way.

The result is that when there is need to part with these metals, which others give up as painfully as if their vitals were being torn out, none of the Utopians regard it as any more than the loss of a penny, so to speak. They find pearls on their shores and diamonds and carbuncles on certain rocks, but they do not search for them. If they find them by chance, they polish them and adorn their younger children with them. As children they take pride and pleasure in such ornaments, and consequently put them aside when they are older and observe that only children use such baubles. This results from their own sense of propriety and not from their parents' commands, just as our children throw away their nuts, amulets, and dolls, when they grow up.

Different customs and institutions produce quite different ideas and attitudes, a truth I never saw better illustrated than in the behavior of the Anemolian [17] ambassadors, who came to Amaurot while I was there. Because they came to discuss important business, three citizens from each city had come to Amaurot ahead of time. The ambassadors from neighboring states, at least those who had been there before, knew that fine clothing was not esteemed among the Utopians, that silk was scorned, and that gold was considered a shameful thing. They came as plainly clothed as possible. But when the Anemolians, who lived far away and had little intercourse with the Utopians, saw that all the people wore the same coarse clothing, they took it for granted that they did not have anything else. They themselves, being a proud rather than a wise people, decided to dress themselves gloriously like gods and dazzle the eyes of the poor Utopians by the splendor of their garb. The three ambassadors made their entry accompanied by a hundred attendants, all dressed in varicolored clothing, many in silk. Since they were nobles at home, the ambassadors wore cloaks of cloth of gold, necklaces and earrings of gold, gold rings on their fingers, caps hung with gold chains studded with pearls and other jewels, in short decked out with all those things which among the Utopians.

17. From the Greek *anemolios*, windy.

were considered badges of slavery, signs of punishment, or toys for children. It was a sight to see how high they held their heads when they compared their clothing with that of the Utopians, for the people had swarmed out into the streets. It was no less amusing to think how far they were from creating the impression which they had expected to make, for in the eyes of all the Utopians, except for those few who had visited other states, all this pomp and splendor seemed shameful. The Utopians saluted all the lowest people as lords and paid no respect at all to the ambassadors themselves, because they seemed to be dressed as slaves with their gold chains. And you might have seen children, who had already thrown away their pearls and gems, nudge their mothers upon seeing the jewels in the ambassadors' caps, and say, "Look, mother! See that big fool who wears pearls and gems, as if he were a little boy!" Then she would say seriously, "Hush, my boy. I think he is one of the ambassadors' fools." Others found fault with the golden chains for being useless and so light that any slave might break them, and so loose that a person when he wished could shake them off, and run away. But after the ambassadors had spent one day and then another there, and had seen the great quantity of cheap gold and silver which was scorned as much by the Utopians as it was held in respect by the Anemolians, and when they had learned also that there was more gold and silver in the chains and fetters of a single slave than in the apparel of all three ambassadors, then their feathers fell. Somewhat shamefacedly they laid aside all the finery in which they had strutted, but they did so willingly, as they had conversed with the Utopians and learned their customs and ideas.

THEIR MORAL PHILOSOPHY

The Utopians wonder that there is any man who delights in the faint gleam of a little gem when he can look at some star or even the sun itself. They marvel that there is any man so foolish as to think himself the nobler because of the fine texture of his woolen clothing. No matter how fine the thread, a sheep once wore it, and the sheep was a sheep still for all its wearing it. They wonder that gold, so useless a thing in itself, is everywhere so highly esteemed that man himself, through whom and by whose use it obtains its value, should be less revered than it. And they do not understand why a blockhead with no more brains than a post, and bad as well as stupid, should have many wise and good men serving him, only because he happens to own a great sum of gold. If he should lose all his money to some utterly worthless fellow in his household, either by some chance or by a legal trick (which can produce changes as great as chance does), he would soon become one of this fellow's servants, as though he belonged to the money and was bound to follow its fortune. But still more the Utopians scorn the folly of those who pay almost divine honors to a rich man, though they owe him nothing and do not fear him, and in fact have no reason for respecting him except that he is rich, and all the while they may know that he is so greedy and grasping that as long as he lives he will never give them a single penny from his great pile of money.

The Utopians have absorbed these and similar attitudes partly from their education, for they are brought up amidst customs and institutions quite opposed to such folly. They have also acquired these notions from their learning and literature. Only a few in each city are excused from labor to devote themselves to learning; these are persons who show an extraordinary capacity and disposition for learning in boyhood. But all the boys are given an education, and a large part of the people, both men and women, spend their leisure hours in reading throughout their lives.

They do all their reading in their own language, which is copious in words, pleasant in sound, and excellent for the expression of thought. The same language prevails over all that part of the world, though it is not equally pure in all places.

Before our arrival, the Utopians had never heard of those philosophers whose names are so celebrated in our part of the world. Yet in music, logic, arithmetic, and geometry they have found out essentially the same things that these great men of old discovered. Thus they equal the ancients in almost everything, but they are far behind our modern logicians. For they have not yet invented the subtle distinctions and hypotheses which have been so cleverly worked out in our trifling schools of logic and taught to the boys here. Nor have they progressed to an understanding of "secondary notions." Not a single one of them was able to see man-in-general (as the logicians call him), though I pointed straight at him with my finger and he is (as you know) bigger than any giant and plainly colossal. On the other hand they

thoroughly understand the course of the stars and the motions of
the heavenly spheres. They have contrived various instruments
for computing exactly the course and position of the sun, moon,
and the other heavenly bodies visible in their part of the sky. As
for the fraud of divining by the stars and attributing friendly or
hostile influences to the planets, they have never thought of it.
From long experience in observation they foretell rainstorms,
winds, and other changes in the weather. About the causes of
these things, and of the sea's tides and saltiness, and about the
origin and nature of earth and sky, they sometimes consider the
same ideas that our ancient philosophers held. And just as our
ancient philosophers differed among themselves, so the Utopian
thinkers differ when they discuss new theories.

In their moral philosophy, they argue much as we do. They
consider what things are truly good, both for the body and the
mind, and whether it is proper to call external things good or
only the gifts of the mind. They inquire into the nature of virtue
and pleasure. But their chief concern is about human happiness,
whether it consists of one thing or of many. They seem much inclined to the view that all or most of human happiness lies in
pleasure. And what may seem strange, they seek support for their
pleasure philosophy from religion, which is serious and stern,
somewhat severe and forbidding. For they never discuss happiness without combining the rational principles of philosophy
with principles taken from religion. They think any inquiry concerning true happiness weak and defective unless it is based on
religion.

The religious principles are these: that the soul of man is immortal and by divine beneficence has been ordained for happiness; and after this life there are rewards appointed for our virtues
and good works and punishment for our sins. They think that
although these beliefs belong to religion, it is in accordance with
reason that they be held and acknowledged. They do not hesitate
to assert that if these were rejected, no one would be so stupid as
not to discern that he ought to seek pleasure regardless of right
and wrong. A man would only need to take care not to let a lesser
pleasure stand in the way of the greater, and not to pursue a
pleasure which brings sorrow in its train. From this point of
view, it is sheer madness to pursue virtue, which seems hard and
harsh, and to give up the pleasures of life and endure pain willingly, and all for nothing. For what can one hope for after a life

without pleasure, that is, after a miserable life, if there is no reward after death?

The Utopians do not believe that there is happiness in all
pleasures, but only in good and honest pleasures. To such, they
believe, our nature is drawn as to its highest good by virtue itself.
The opposite point of view is that happiness consists of virtue
alone.

They define virtue as living according to nature. We have been
ordained, they say, by God to this end. To follow nature is to
conform to the dictates of reason in what we seek and avoid. The
first dictate of reason is ardently to love and revere the Divine
Majesty, to whom we owe what we are and whatever happiness
we can reach. Secondly, reason warns us and summons us to lead
our lives as calmly and cheerfully as we can, and to help all
others in nature's fellowship to attain this good.

They disagree with the grim and gloomy eulogist of virtue,
who hates pleasure and exhorts us to toils and vigils and squalid
self-denial, and at the same time commands us to relieve the
poverty and lighten the burdens of others in accordance with our
humanity. He proclaims that this is the glory of human nature,
to mitigate the sufferings of others and restore the joys of living—
that is, pleasure—by driving grief away. If this is true, the Utopians argue, does it not follow that nature incites us to do the
same for ourselves? If a joyful life (that is, one of pleasure) is
bad, then we ought not to help others to it; on the contrary we
ought to keep them from it. But if a joyful life is good, and if we
are supposed to help others to enjoy one, why should we not seek
such a life for ourselves as much as for others? For nature does
not teach us to be harsh and cruel to ourselves while being kind
and helpful to each other.

So they conclude that nature herself prescribes a life of joy
(that is, of pleasure) as the goal of life. This is what they mean
by saying that virtue is living according to nature. And as nature
bids us mutually to make our lives merry and delightful, so she
also bids us again and again not to destroy or diminish other
people's pleasure in seeking our own. And in this they think
nature is quite right. No one is so much above the rest of mankind that he is nature's sole care. She cherishes all alike whom she
embraces in the community of the same form.

Consequently they believe that men should keep their private
agreements, and should obey those public laws which a good

ruler has justly decreed or which the people, influenced neither by force nor fraud, have freely sanctioned. For such laws determine the distribution of goods, and goods are a prerequisite of pleasure.

They think it is prudent for a man to pursue his own advantage so far as the laws allow, but they account it as piety for him to prefer the public good to his own. It is wrong for a man to seek his own pleasure by thwarting another's; but to decrease his own to add to the pleasure of others they count a work of humanity and benevolence, and one, moreover, which benefits him as much as he benefits others. For in time of need he may be repaid for his kindness. Even if this never happens, his awareness that he did a good deed and the recollection of the gratitude of those whom he benefited will delight his mind more than the pleasure he gave up would have pleased his body. Finally they believe what religion easily persuades a well-disposed mind to believe, that God repays the loss of a short and transitory pleasure with great and endless joy.

Thus after weighing the matter carefully, they conclude that all our actions, and among these our virtues, ultimately look toward pleasure and happiness as their end. They call pleasure all the acts and states of body or mind in which man naturally delights. But they include in their concept of pleasure only those appetites to which nature leads us. And they maintain that nature leads us only to the delights approved by right reason as well as by the senses, that is, only those delights by which we neither injure others, nor lose a greater pleasure for a less, nor suffer for later. Those attractions which are inconsistent with nature and which men call delights only by the emptiest of fictions (as if men could change their nature by changing their name), these things they say diminish happiness rather than increase it. For men whose minds are filled up with a false idea of pleasure have no room left for true pleasures and genuine delight.

There are many things that in themselves contain nothing delightful, but on the contrary have no little bitterness about them. Yet from the perverse enticement of evil desires, they are esteemed not only as very great pleasures, but even as the most urgent goals in life. Among those who pursue this kind of false pleasure, the Utopians include the men I mentioned who think themselves better for having finer clothes. Such men are twice mistaken. They are no less mistaken in thinking their clothes are better than other men's clothes than they are in thinking that they themselves are better. If you consider the use of clothes, why is wool made of fine thread better than wool made of coarse thread? Yet these men carry their heads high and think they are somehow superior, as if they excelled by nature and not by wrong opinion. So they require in their own right the honor which they would not expect if they were poorly dressed, and are indignant if they are slighted.

It is the same kind of folly to be pleased by the useless marks of outward respect. What natural or true pleasure can you get, if some one bares his head to you or bends his knees? Will the pain in your knees be eased thereby, or the madness in your head? The same mistaken ideas of pleasure are held by men who flatter and applaud themselves for their ancient ancestry and especially for their rich estates (for nothing but wealth makes nobility at present). Yet they do not think themselves a whit less noble, even if these ancestors left them nothing, or if they themselves have squandered their inheritance.

In the same class the Utopians put those who are enamored of gems and jewelry, and who think themselves divinely happy if they obtain some rare gem highly prized in their country at the time (for stones vary in value at different times and among various people). They will not buy the gem until it is dismounted from its gold setting and until the seller has sworn to put up security that it is genuine, because they are afraid that their eyes will be deceived by a counterfeit. But if you consider it, why will a counterfeit gem furnish you any less pleasure, if your eyes cannot distinguish it from a genuine one? They are of equal worth to you, as truly as if you were blind!

Then there are those who pile up wealth, not for any use but only for the pleasure of looking at it. Do they enjoy any true pleasure, or are they deceived, instead, by false pleasure? What of those others who hide away wealth which they are never going to use and perhaps never even see again? In their anxiety to keep it, they actually lose it. That is really what happens when a man takes it away from himself and also from the rest of mankind, and returns it to the earth. Yet when he has hidden the treasure, he feels sure of it and is happy. Now suppose it is stolen, and that the owner does not discover the theft until ten years later. In all that time what does it matter whether the money has been stolen or not? In either case it is equally useless to him.

To these foolish pleasures they add gambling (which they know only by hearsay) and hunting and fowling. What pleasure is it, they say, to throw dice? If there were any pleasure in it, would not throwing them over and over again make one tire of it? What pleasure can there be in hearing the barking and howling of dogs? Why is a dog chasing a hare more enjoyable than a dog chasing a dog? For the same thing is done in each case, that is running—if that is so enjoyable. But if a man hopes to see the hare torn to pieces before his eyes, he ought instead to pity the timid harmless hare, fleeing from a fierce dog only to be torn to pieces by the cruel beast in the end. So the Utopians, regarding this whole business of hunting as a thing unworthy of free men, turn it over to their butchers, who (as I have said) are bondmen. They count hunting as the lowest kind of butcher work. It is more useful and honorable to keep cattle and kill them only when needed. But a hunter seeks sheer pleasure from the slaughter and mutilation of some small helpless animal. They think this enjoyment in beholding deaths, even in beasts, comes from an inherently cruel disposition or from the habitual practice of cruelty in so brutal a pleasure.

The Utopians maintain that these and countless other things which the mass of mankind regard as pleasure have nothing to do with it, since they are not at all delightful by nature. They often please the senses (and in this are like pleasures), but that makes no difference. They are not pleasing in themselves, but only because of man's corrupt customs. Men accept the bitter as sweet, just as pregnant women think pitch and tallow taste sweeter than honey. Whether affected by sickness or influenced by custom, a person's taste cannot change the essential qualities of anything. No more can it change the nature of pleasure.

They discriminate several kinds of true pleasures, some belonging to the mind, others to the body. Those of the mind are knowledge and the delight which comes from contemplation of the truth; also the pleasant recollection of a well-spent life and the assured hope of future well-being.

They divide bodily pleasures into two sorts. The first kind is that which fills the senses with immediate pleasure. This occurs when the body's parts are renewed and refreshed by food and drink, or when some excess in the body is discharged, as in bowel movements, procreation, or rubbing and scratching some itch.

There is a second kind of bodily pleasure that neither repairs nor relieves our bodies, but excites our senses with some hidden but unmistakable force and turns them inwardly upon themselves. Such is the pleasure that comes from music.

Another form of bodily pleasure consists of a quiet, sound condition of the body, its general well-being when disturbed by no disease. This condition in itself gives inward pleasure, though it is not excited by anything external. Although it affects the senses less strongly than the obvious satisfaction of eating and drinking, yet many count this the greater pleasure. Most of the Utopians say that this is the foundation of all pleasures, since it alone makes a calm and desirable condition. If it is lacking, there is no chance for any other pleasure. Mere absence of pain they call insensibility, not pleasure, unless it is a state of health.

In times past they carried on a vigorous controversy as to whether assured and tranquil health is really a pleasure, since it only makes itself felt when it is threatened by its opposite. Today they all agree that health is the greatest of all bodily pleasures. Just as pain is inherent in sickness, they argue, so pleasure (the opposite of pain) is inherent in the opposite condition, namely good health. If it is said that sickness is not a pain, but merely has pain in it, they say this makes no difference. For whether health is itself a pleasure or is merely the cause of pleasure (as fire is of heat), whoever is healthy has true pleasure in it. When we eat, they say, what happens is that our health, which began to weaken, fights against hunger with food as its ally. In this struggle as we gradually gain strength and recover our vigor, we feel the pleasure of being refreshed. And will not our health, which felt delight during the conflict, rejoice in the victory it has won? When our health regains complete vitality, will it not be sensible of its well-being? Thus they maintain that good health can be felt. If a man is not sick, he feels that he is well when he is awake. Is any man so dull or lethargic as not to admit that health feels delightful? And what is delight but another name for pleasure?

Of all the pleasures they especially embrace those of the mind, for they esteem them most highly, thinking they arise from the exercise of the virtues and from the consciousness of a good life. Among bodily pleasures they give first place to health. They hold that the pleasure of eating and drinking and all other delights of the body are desirable only as they maintain health. They are not delightful in themselves, but only as they resist the encroachments of sickness. A wise man thinks it better to ward off sickness than to seek medicine, and to overcome troubles rather than to seek comfort. So it is better to reject these pleasures of sense than to be captivated by them. If any man thinks he is happy in the midst of these pleasures, then he must confess that he would be the happiest of men if he should spend his whole life in an unending round of hunger, thirst, itching, followed by eating, drinking, scratching and rubbing. Who cannot see that such a life is not only vile, but miserable? These are the lowest of all pleasures, and the least pure, for they are always mixed with contrary pains; as hunger is tied up with the pleasure of eating, and the pain outweighs the pleasure. The pain is not only stronger, but lasts longer, for it comes before the pleasure and does not end until the pleasure ends along with it. So the Utopians think pleasures of this sort are not to be highly valued, except in so far as they are necessary to life. Yet they rejoice in them, and gratefully recognize the kindness of Mother Nature, who lures her children with such blandishments toward what is necessary for existence. How miserable life would be if daily hunger and thirst had to be overcome by bitter potions and drugs, as are other ills that afflict us less often! But instead, these pleasant and appropriate gifts of nature readily sustain the beauty, strength, and agility of the body.

The Utopians also pursue the pleasures of sound, sight, and smell, and think that they give savor and relish to human life. Nature seems to have intended these pleasures peculiarly for man. No other kind of animal contemplates the comeliness and beauty of the universe, or takes pleasure in odors except to distinguish foods, or recognizes concords and discords of sounds. But in all their pleasures the Utopians observe this rule, that a lesser pleasure shall not stand in the way of a greater and that pleasure shall not breed pain. They believe that pain necessarily follows false pleasure.

Moreover they think it madness for a man to mar his body, to weaken his strength, to make himself sluggish, to wear himself down with fasts, to ruin his health, and spurn natural delights, unless by neglecting his own satisfaction he can better serve the welfare of others or the public good, for which in return he expects a greater reward from God. Such a man does no one any good. He gains only the empty shadow of virtue, or hardens himself against adversities which may never come. They consider him cruel to himself and ungrateful to nature, whose blessings he refuses as if he disdained to be indebted to her.

These are their ideas of virtue and pleasure, and they think that human reason can find none truer, unless some heavenly revelation should inspire more sublime ideas in men. I have no time now to consider whether they are right in these views or not, nor do I think it necessary, as I only undertook to give an account of their customs, not to defend them. Whatever the validity of these principles, I am sure that nowhere is there a more excellent people or a happier commonwealth.

In body they are agile and lively, and stronger than their size suggests. Though their soil is not very fertile nor their air the most wholesome, they fortify themselves against their air by temperate living and improve their soil by industry, so that nowhere is there a greater yield of grain and cattle and nowhere are men more vigorous or subject to fewer diseases. You may see them diligently doing what farmers usually do to improve poor soil by skill and labor, and even rooting up a forest from one place and planting it in another. This is not done for the sake of fertility, but to aid transportation, that firewood may be near the sea or rivers or their cities. For it is less work to transport grain a long distance by land than wood. They are quick to learn, good-natured, dexterous, and fond of leisure. They are able to endure labor when it is necessary, but are otherwise not very fond of it.

THEIR DELIGHT IN LEARNING

In intellectual pursuits they are tireless. When they heard us speak of the literature and learning of the Greeks (for we thought there was nothing among the Romans they would value much except the historians and poets), it was wonderful to see how eagerly they sought to be instructed in Greek. We began to read a little of it to them rather because of their importunity than because of any expectation on our part that they would profit from it. But after a short trial, we saw by their diligence that our efforts would not be wasted. For they began to copy the forms of the letters so readily, to pronounce the language so correctly, and to memorize it so quickly and accurately, that it would have seemed miraculous, had not most of those whom we taught been men of unusual ability and mature years. Some studied with us of their own accord, while others were selected from among their learned men by the senate. In less than three years they were able to read the best Greek authors easily, unless hindered by textual flaws. I am inclined to think that they learned this language more readily because their speech, while generally nearer the Persian, retains some remnants of Greek speech in the names of cities and magistrates.

When I was about to sail on my fourth voyage, I put on board a good-sized pack of books in place of merchandise, because I was so far from expecting to return soon that I thought I might never return. Thus they received from me many of Plato's works, and still more of Aristotle's; Theophrastus's *On Plants,* too, which I am sorry to say was mutilated in several places, for while at sea I rather carelessly laid it down and a playful monkey found it and mischievously tore some pages here and there. Of grammarians they received only Lascaris, for I did not take Theodorus with me, nor any dictionary except Hesychius and Dioscorides. They were very fond of the books of Plutarch and were charmed with the wit and grace of Lucian. Of the poets they now have Aristophanes, Homer, and Euripides, as well as Sophocles in the Aldine edition. Among historians they have Thucydides and Herodotus, also Herodian. As for medical works, a companion of mine, Tricius Apinatus,[18] had brought with him some short works of Hippocrates, and Galen's *Microtechne.* These works on medicine they prize very highly, because though they need medical science least of all people, none hold it in greater honor, and they count medicine among the most pleasant and profitable parts of natural science. In their study of nature's secrets, they not only find wonderful pleasure for themselves, but they believe that they please the Author and Maker of nature. For they think that, in the manner of other artificers, He has exposed this machine of the universe to man's view because man alone is able to contemplate it, and that therefore a careful observer and eager admirer of His workmanship is dearer to Him than a dull and unmoved being who looks upon this great spectacle like an animal incapable of thought.

18. The name is a reference to Martial, I, cxiv, 2, and XIV, i, 7. It is equivalent to "Mr. Playful Nonsense." The joke in no way implies disrespect for the works of Hippocrates and Galen.

The minds of the Utopians, when once stimulated by learning, are uncommonly quick in such inventions as increase the conveniences of life. Two of these, printing and the making of paper, they owe partly to us, partly to their own ingenuity. After we had showed them some paper books from the Aldus press and spoke of the method of making paper and printing on it, not really explaining it (for none of us were experienced in either one), they immediately grasped the principles involved. While heretofore they had written only on skins, bark, or reeds, they now undertook to make paper and to print letters. The results were not quite satisfactory at first. But after some trials they soon achieved success in both arts. If they had texts of other Greek authors, they would soon have plenty of copies. They have already printed thousands of copies of the books I have mentioned.

They welcome anyone to their country who has some unusual ability or who has learned the customs of many peoples. (This is why we were so well received). For they are eager to know what is going on everywhere in the world. However, very few merchants go there to trade. For what can a man bring there except iron, or else gold and silver (which men prefer to keep rather than to export)? As for the Utopians' exports, they think it preferable to do their own exporting rather than have it done by others. In this way they are able to know the neighboring peoples better and to keep up their skill in navigation.

THEIR BONDMEN

They do not make bondmen of prisoners of war, except those whom they themselves capture. They do not enslave the sons of their bondmen, nor any who were slaves among other nations. Their bondmen are either their own citizens who have been sentenced to bondage for some crime, or men of other nations who have been condemned to death. The Utopians buy these men at a low price, or more often obtain them free of charge and bring them home.

All kinds of bondmen are kept constantly at work and are always chained. The Utopians treat their native bondmen more harshly than the others, thinking them baser and deserving of greater punishment, because they could not be restrained from crime in spite of their excellent education and moral training. Another class of bondmen consists of poor, hard-working menials of some other nation, who have chosen of their own accord to come and serve the Utopians. They are treated well, almost as kindly as citizens, except that they are given somewhat more work, and to this these foreigners are accustomed. If, as is seldom the case, they wish to leave, they are not detained against their will, nor are they sent away empty-handed.

THEIR CARE OF THE SICK AND EUTHANASIA

The sick, as I have said, they tend carefully, omitting no medicine or food that will restore them to health. They relieve those who suffer from some incurable disease by sitting and talking with them and by alleviating their pain in every possible way. But if a person suffers from a disease which is both incurable and continually excruciating, the priests and magistrates come and urge him to make the decision not to nourish such a painful disease any longer. He is now unequal to all the duties of life, a burden to himself and to others, having really outlived himself. They tell him not to hesitate to die when life is such a torment, but in confidence of a better life after death, to deliver himself from the scourge and imprisonment of living or let others release him. This, they say, he would do wisely, for by death he would lose nothing but suffering. Since he would be acting on the advice of the priests, who are the interpreters of God's will, he would act rightly and virtuously. Those who are moved by these arguments either starve themselves to death of their own accord or through the aid of an opiate die painlessly. If a man is not persuaded to this course, they do not force him to it against his will, nor do they lessen their care of him. To choose death under these circumstances is honorable. But they dishonor a man who takes his own life without the approval of the priests and senate. They consider him unworthy of decent burial and throw his body unburied and disgraced into a ditch.

THEIR MARRIAGE CUSTOMS

A woman is not married before eighteen, nor a man before twenty-two. If a man (or woman) is convicted of an illict affair before marriage, he is severely punished and marriage is denied him for his whole life, unless a prince's pardon remits the punishment. The master and mistress of the household in which the offense has occured are in disgrace for having been remiss in their duty. The reason for punishing this offense so severely is the fear that few would unite in married love, to spend their whole lives with one person and put up with all the annoyances of marriage, unless they were rigorously restrained from promiscuity.

In the choice of wives they carefully follow a custom which seemed to us foolish and absurd. Before marriage some responsible and honorable woman, either a virgin or a widow, presents the woman naked to her suitor and after that some upright man presents the suitor naked to the woman. We laughed at this and condemned it as foolish. On the contrary they wonder at the stupidity of other people, who are exceedingly cautious in matters involving only a little money. For example, men will refuse to buy a colt, unless they take off its saddle and harness, which might conceal a sore. But in the choice of a mate, on which one's happiness depends for the rest of one's life, they act carelessly. They leave all but a hand's-breadth of the woman's face covered with clothing and judge her by it, so that in marrying a couple runs a great risk of mutual dislike if later anything in either's body should offend the other. Not all men are so wise that they consider only a woman's behavior. And even wise men think that physical beauty in wives adds not a little to the virtues of the mind. Certainly some deformity may lurk underneath clothing which will alienate a man from his wife when it is too late to be separated from her. If such a deformity is discovered after marriage, a man must bear his lot, so the Utopians think care ought to be taken by law that no one be deceived.

There is all the more reason for their taking this precaution, because in that part of the world they alone are monogamists. Their marriages are broken only by death. They do not allow divorce except for adultery or insufferable waywardness on the part of either spouse. The injured person is given permission to change spouses by the senate, but the guilty party is considered disreputable and for the rest of his life is forbidden to remarry. They do not allow a husband to put away his wife against her will because of some bodily misfortune. They consider it a matter of cruelty and disloyalty to desert one's spouse when most in need of comfort, especially in old age (which is itself really a sickness, since it brings sickness in its train). It happens occasionally that when a married couple cannot agree well together and when they have found other persons with whom they hope to live more happily, they separate by mutual consent and contract new marriages, but only with the consent of the senate. Such divorces are not allowed unless the senators and their wives have made careful inquiry into the grounds for it. They allow them unwillingly, for they know that it weakens the love of married couples to leave the door open to easy new marriages.

They punish adulterers with the severest bondage. If both parties are married, they are divorced, and the injured persons may be married to one another or to some one else. But if either of the injured parties continues to love the undeserving spouse, then the couple may live together in marriage, provided the innocent person is willing to share in the labor to which bondmen are condemned. Sometimes it happens that the repentance of the guilty person so moves the prince to pity that he grants both of them freedom once more. If anyone commits adultery a second time, his punishment is death.

THEIR PUNISHMENTS, THEIR LEGAL PROCEDURE, AND OTHER MATTERS

Their law lays down no other fixed penalties, but the senate fixes the punishment according to the wickedness of the crime. Husbands punish their wives, and parents their children, unless the offense is so great that a public punishment seems to be for the common good. Generally the most serious crimes are punished by bondage, for they think this no less terrible to criminals than death. And it is more beneficial to the commonwealth, for a bondman's labor is worth more to the state than his death. Moreover the sight of bondage longer deters other men from similar crimes. If bondmen rebel and refuse to work, they are put to death like wild beasts which neither captivity nor chains can restrain. Those who bear their bondage patiently are not left hopeless. After they have been tamed by long hardship, if they show by their repentance that their wrongdoing troubles them more than their punishment, their bondage is modified or remitted, sometimes by the prince's prerogative and sometimes by popular vote.

A man who attempts to seduce a woman risks the same punishment as if he had actually done it. They think that an attempted crime is as bad as one committed, and that a man's failure should not mitigate his punishment when he did all he could to succeed.

They take pleasure in fools. While they think it contemptible to mistreat them, they do not forbid men to enjoy their foolishness, and even regard this as beneficial to the fools. No fools are entrusted to the care of serious and stern men who do not laugh at their ridiculous behavior and jests, for fear that a man who finds no enjoyment in a fool's only gift will not treat him kindly.

To jeer at a person for being deformed or crippled is not considered a reproach to him. But the mocker, who stupidly upbraids the cripple for something he cannot help, is held in contempt.

They consider it a sign of sluggish disposition to neglect one's natural beauty, but they think it is detestable to use rouge. They have learned by experience that no physical beauty recommends a wife to her husband as much as uprightness and obedience. Though some men are won by beauty, none are held except by virtue and compliance.

They deter men from crime by penalties and incite them to virtue by public honors. They set up statues of distinguished men who have deserved well of their country in the market places, to preserve the memory of their good deeds and to spur on the citizens to emulate the glory of their ancestors.

Any man who campaigns too zealously for a magistracy is sure to fail. They live together harmoniously and the magistrates are never proud or cruel. Instead they are called fathers, and deservedly. Because the magistrates do not exact honor from the people against their will, the people honor them willingly, as they should. Not even the prince has the distinction of robe or diadem; he is known only by a sheaf of grain carried before him. In the same way the priest is known by a wax candle.

They have few laws, and such are their institutions that they need few. They strongly censure other nations, which cannot get along without an infinite number of laws and interpretations.

They think it highly unjust to bind men by laws that are too numerous to be read and too obscure to be readily understood. As for lawyers, a kind of men who handle matters craftily and interpret laws subtly, they have none at all. They maintain that it is better for each man to plead his own case, and to entrust to the judge what he would elsewhere tell his lawyer. Thus there is less delay, and the truth is brought out more readily. A man speaks without the help of a lawyer's wily instruction, and the judge examines each point carefully, and protects the simpler sort against the falsehoods of crafty men. It is hard to find such equitable procedure among other nations, with their multitude of intricate laws.

But in Utopia everyone is skillful in the law. For the laws are very few, as I have said, and the plainest interpretation is the fairest. All laws, according to their view, are promulgated for the single purpose of teaching each man his duty. Subtle interpretations teach very few, for there are few who can understand them; the simpler and more obvious sense of the laws is clear to all. If laws are not clear, they are useless for the masses of people who need their guidance most. There might as well be no laws at all as to have laws which only men of great ability and long training can interpret. Most men lack the brains for this task and cannot spare the time from their work.

THEIR FOREIGN RELATIONS

In times past the Utopians have helped some of their neighbors gain freedom from tyrants. These people admire the virtues of the Utopians so much that of their own accord they have asked the Utopians to send men to be their rulers. Some of these rulers serve for a year, others for five. When their term is finished, they come back bringing with them praise and esteem, and others are sent in their place. These nations seem to have found an excellent plan for their happiness and safety. As the welfare or evil of a state depends on the moral character of its magistrates, what men could they choose more wisely than these, who cannot be tempted by money? For money is useless to them when they go home. And because they are not natives, they are not swayed by rivalries and strife. When these two evils, avarice and partiality, afflict judges, they are the destruction of all justice, which is the chief

bond of society. The Utopians call those people that seek magistrates from them neighbors, and those whom they have aided
still more, friends.

Whereas other nations are continually making alliances, breaking them, and then renewing them, the Utopians make no alliances with any nation. If nature, they say, will not make man
friendly with man, will an alliance do so? Will a man who scorns
nature respect mere words? They have been confirmed in this
view all the more, because among neighboring nations the alliances and pacts of princes are usually so carelessly observed.

In Europe, especially where the Christian religion prevails,
treaty agreements are sacred and inviolable. This is partly owing
to the justice and goodness of princes, and partly to the reverence
and fear they feel toward the popes, who themselves observe their
agreements very religiously. The popes order all other chiefs of
state to abide by their promises, even bringing pressure upon
evaders by pontifical censure. And the popes rightly point out
that it would be most ignominious if men who are specifically
called "the faithful" were faithless to their treaties.

But in this new world, which is as far from us in distance as
our customs are different from theirs, no confidence is put in
alliances, even though they are contracted with the most sacred
ceremonies. The greater the formalities, the sooner the treaty may
be dissolved by twisting the words, which are often purposely
ambiguous. A treaty can never be bound with chains so strong,
but that a government can somehow evade it and thereby break
both the treaty and its faith. If statesmen found such craftiness
and fraud in the contracts of business men, they would scornfully brand them as sacrilegious and worthy of the gallows. These
very statesmen, however, take pride in giving just such counsel
to princes. Thus justice seems to be a low and humble virtue, one
which dwells far beneath the high dignity of kings. Or there may
be two kinds of justice, one the people's justice, mean, lowly,
bound by fetters on every side so that it cannot jump the fences,
the other the justice of princes, which is more majestic and so
much freer than the other that it may take whatever it wants.

This practice of keeping treaties so badly is the reason why the
Utopians make no alliances. They might indeed change their
minds if they lived here. However, they think it a bad custom
to make treaties at all, even if they are well observed. To do so
makes it seem as if men who are separated by only a hill or a

river were bound by no tie of nature, but were born natural enemies and therefore rightly attacked each other unless restrained by treaties. Moreover they see that these alliances do not cement friendship; the two countries still have licence to prey upon each other, unless sufficient caution is used in making the treaty to see that there is no loophole in the wording. The Utopians' view is that no man should be esteemed an enemy if he has done no injury, that the fellowship of nature among men serves instead of a treaty, and that men are bound more adequately by good will than by pacts, more strongly by their hearts than by their words.

THEIR WARFARE

They hate and detest war as a thing manifestly brutal, and yet practiced by man more constantly than by any kind of beast. Contrary to almost all other peoples they consider nothing so inglorious as the glory won in war. Nevertheless both the men and the women of Utopia regularly practice military exercises on certain days, so that they will be prepared when the need arises. They go to war cautiously and reluctantly, only to protect their own territory or that of their friends if an enemy has invaded it, or to free some wretched people from tyrannous oppression and servitude. They help their friends not only in defense, but also to avenge injuries. They do this only if they are consulted in the whole affair, if the facts are proved, and if the stolen plunder is not returned. Then they think they should wage war against the aggressor. They decide on this policy when booty is taken from their friends by force or when the merchants of one country are oppressed in another country by unjust laws or by twisting good laws. This they think is a greater evil than direct attack.

This was the sole cause of the war which the Utopians waged against the Alaopolitans for the sake of the Nephelogetes [19] some time before our arrival, when a wrong seemed to have been done under pretext of right to Nephelogete merchants resident among the Alaopolitans. Whether or not an injustice was done, it was avenged by a terrible war, the strength of each side being augmented by the resources and the hatred of their neighbors. Some prosperous nations were ruined and others were greatly shaken.

19. "The Men of Dark City" and "The Cloudlanders" respectively.

In the end after a series of misfortunes, the Alaopolitans, who had been a very thriving people compared to the Nephelogetes, were conquered and reduced to bondage by the Nephelogetes. Vigorously as the Utopians stood by their friends in the matter of reparations, they sought none for themselves.

If the Utopians themselves are cheated in this way, they carry their anger only to the point of cutting off trade with that country, provided no bodily injury is done. Not that they care less for their own citizens than for their neighbors, but they think it worse for their neighbors' property to be seized than their own. Their neighbors' merchants suffer a great injury because they lose their own property, but the Utopians think little of their loss, for only common goods have been lost. Besides whatever is exported must be in superfluous abundance at home, or it would not be shipped out. So they think it cruel to avenge a relatively unimportant loss by killing many men, whose death would only affect the lives and livelihood of others. But if any Utopian citizens are unjustly hurt or killed, whether by private or public policy, they send envoys demanding that the guilty persons be handed over to them. If that is refused, they declare war. If the guilty men are given up, their punishment is death or bondage.

The Utopians are troubled and ashamed when they gain a bloody victory, like merchants who have paid too high a price for what they have bought. If they overwhelm the enemy by skill and cunning, they exult and celebrate a public triumph, and erect a memorial for a victory efficiently won. When they win a victory by the strength of understanding (as only men can), they pride themselves on acting bravely and manfully. Bears, lions, boars, wolves, dogs, and other wild beasts fight with their bodies, and many of them surpass us in strength and ferocity as much as we surpass them in understanding and reason.

The Utopians have this one aim in war, to accomplish what they would gladly have achieved without war if just terms had been granted in time. Or if that cannot be done, they aim to exact so severe a revenge from those that have injured them that they will be afraid to do it again. Their policies are directed to these ends, which they strive toward in such a way as to avoid danger rather than to attain glory and fame.

As soon as war is declared, they at once arrange to have many small notices, which are marked with their official seal, set up by stealth in the most conspicuous places in the enemy's country. In these proclamations they promise great rewards to any one who will kill the enemy's king, and smaller rewards (but still very great) for killing those whom they regard as most responsible after the king for plotting aggression against them. They double the reward for anyone who brings in the proscribed man alive. Also they offer like rewards, as well as exemption from punishment, to any of the proscribed men who turn against their countrymen. As a result the proscribed men soon suspect everyone, distrust each other, and become distracted by their danger. It has often turned out that many of them, and even princes, have been betrayed by those whom they most trusted. The Utopians realize that rewards will spur men on to any sort of crime, and consequently they promise incredible gifts. Mindful of the danger which the assassins run, they see to it that the compensation is proportionate to the risk, and promise an immense amount of gold and also rich estates safely placed in neighboring countries. They keep these promises most faithfully. Though this manner of waging war by bidding for and buying enemies may seem like the cruel villainy of an ignoble mind, it is considered by the Utopians as a wise and praiseworthy policy, since it enables them to wage great wars without any battle at all. They even think themselves humane and merciful, because by the death of a few bad men they spare the lives of many innocent men who would otherwise die in battle, some fighting on their own side, some on the enemy's. Indeed they pity the mass of enemy soldiers no less than their own, for they know that they do not fight willingly, but are driven to it by the madness of their rulers.

If this method does not succeed, they sow the seeds of discord among the enemy by inciting the king's brother or some member of the nobility to plot for the crown. If these internal factions languish, then they arouse the neighboring people against the enemy and induce them to revive some old claims, such as kings never lack.

When they promise their resources to help in a war, they furnish money abundantly, but citizens very sparingly. They hold their own men most dear and of such account that they will not willingly exchange one of the citizens for an enemy's king. Since they keep their gold and silver for this single purpose, they spend it without reluctance, the more so as they will live no less well if they spend it all. Besides the wealth which they have at home, they have also boundless treasure abroad, many neighboring nations being in their debt, as I have said. So they hire mercenary soldiers from all sides, especially from the Zapoletes.[20]

These people live five hundred miles from Utopia toward the east. They are a rude, fierce, wild people, who delight in the forests and mountains among which they are brought up. They are sturdy, well able to endure heat, cold, and hard work. They are unacquainted with luxuries or with agriculture, and are indifferent about housing and clothing. Their only productive occupation is taking care of cattle. For the most part they live by hunting and theft. It is as if they were born for war, and they watch carefully for any chance to engage in it. When they find such a chance they eagerly embrace it, great numbers of them going out and offering themselves at a low price to any one seeking soldiers. They know only one art for earning a living, the art of taking away life. They fight for their employers fiercely and with incorruptible fidelity. But they will not bind themselves to serve for any set time. They stipulate that they may fight next day for the enemy, if higher pay is offered, and come back on the day after that for still higher pay. There is seldom a war in which a considerable number of them are not fighting on both sides. So it commonly happens that men who are related to one another by blood and have served together in intimacy in the same campaigns are enlisted on opposite sides. Forgetful of their relationship and their friendship, they kill one another for no other reason than that they have been hired for a paltry wage by different kings. They think so much of money that they will change sides readily for an increase of only a penny a day. Thus they grow greedier and greedier for money, but money is of no use to them, for what they acquire with their blood, they soon waste profligately on contemptible pleasures.

This nation serves the Utopians against all people whatsoever, for they give higher pay than any others. Just as the Utopians seek out the best possible men to use at home, by the same principle they seek the worst men to misuse in war. When need requires, they induce the Zapoletes with promises of rich rewards to face hazards from which most of them never return. The Utopians pay the rewards in good faith to those who escape death, to incite them to similar deeds of daring later. And the Utopians

20. "The Ready-Sellers."

have no concern over how many are killed, thinking they would deserve the thanks of the human race if they could purge the world of the whole of that disgusting and vicious people.

In addition to these, they use the soldiers of the people for whom they are fighting, and the troops of other friends as auxiliaries. Finally they add some of their own citizens, including some man of approved valor to command the entire army. They add two substitutes, who serve as privates while the commander is safe. But if he is captured or killed, one of the two succeeds him, and then in case of a mishap to him, the other. In this way they provide that in the varying fortunes of war the whole army may not be endangered by an accident befalling their leader. For their own soldiers they take men from each city who volunteer freely. No one is forced into service away from home against his will. They think that a man who is naturally timid will act weakly, and even dishearten his companions. But if their own country is invaded, they use even these faint-hearted men, provided they are sound in body. They place them on shipboard among better men, or here and there on fortifications where there is no chance of flight. Shame, the immediate presence of the foe, and the hopelessness of flight overcome their fear, and they often show themselves brave from sheer necessity.

Just as no one is forced to go into a foreign war unwillingly, so women are allowed to follow their husbands to war if they wish and are encouraged and praised for doing so. They place each woman beside her husband in the front line of battle. They also station each man's children, kinsmen, and connections around him in order that those whom nature most incites to help one another may be nearest at hand to give mutual aid. It is considered a matter of great reproach for one spouse to survive the other, or for a son to survive his parent. Therefore when battle is joined, they fight it out in a long and bloody struggle to the last man, if the enemy stands fast.

If possible they use only their mercenaries and so avoid sending their own citizens to battle. When this is impossible and they must take part in the fighting themselves, they join battle with a boldness as great as their prudence in avoiding it. They do not begin with a fierce impulsive charge, but gradually as the fighting goes on they increase in valor, becoming so stubborn that they die rather than yield ground. They are free from the cares which often weaken noble spirits. Their own security at home and their confidence in their children's welfare make them stout-hearted and too proud to be conquered. Moreover their skill in warfare increases their valor, and the sound ideas instilled into them in childhood by instruction and the wise institutions of their commonwealth add to their courage. They do not hold life so cheap that they waste it, nor do they hold it so dear that they avidly and shamefully grasp it when duty bids them give it up.

When the battle rages hottest, the bravest young men, who have joined themselves together by oaths, take upon themselves to destroy the leader of the enemy's forces. They assault him openly, they ambush him, they attack him hand to hand. Fresh men replace those who are worn out in the continuous struggle. In the end they rarely fail to kill or capture him, unless he takes to flight.

When they win a battle, they are more ready to take prisoners than to make a great slaughter. They never pursue fugitives without keeping part of their army in good order arrayed under their standards. If the rest of their army has been overcome and they have only gained the victory with their reserve troops, they think it better to let the enemy slip away with forces intact rather than pursue them with their own ranks in disorder. For they remember what happened more than once to themselves. After the enemy's main army had been overcome, the Utopians, scattered and apprehensive of no danger, were pursuing the retreating foe in the glow of victory. Among this conquered army some few men had been placed in reserve and were watching for their opportunity. Suddenly they attacked and changed the course of the whole battle. The conquered seized the victory from the seeming victors and in turn became the conquerors.

They are equally shrewd in laying ambushes and in avoiding them. Sometimes they seem to be preparing to flee, when their real intention is the opposite. Again, when they are planning flight, you would never guess it. If they think they are too few in number or are in a poor position, they either move camp silently in the night, or slip off by some other stratagem. Or they fall back in the daytime so gradually and in such good order, that it is as dangerous to attack them in their retreat as in their advance.

They fortify their camps very carefully with a wide and very deep trench. They throw the earth inward, where it is used for a wall. They do not use bondmen for this work. The entire army takes part except for those who serve in front of the rampart as an armed guard against sudden attack. With so many hands at work they complete great fortifications around a large area in an incredibly short time.

The armor they use is strong for resisting blows, but does not interfere with their bodily movements. In fact, they can even swim in it. Part of their training in warfare is learning to swim in armor. For fighting at a distance they use arrows, which both infantry and cavalry shoot with speed and sureness. For close fighting their weapons are not swords but sharp and heavy axes used with a forward lunge or a downstroke. They devise ingenious engines of war and then keep them well hidden, for fear that if these were known before they were needed and if the enemy discovered them, they would be useless except as a butt for the enemy's jokes. In designing them, the first consideration is that they may be easily carried and manipulated.

When the Utopians agree to a truce, they observe it so religiously that they will not violate it even though provoked. They do not lay waste the enemy's country nor burn his grain. In their marches they take care that neither the men nor the horses trample down the grain, for they may need it themselves. They attack no man who is disarmed unless he is a spy. When cities are surrendered, they take them under their protection. If they carry a place by storm, they do not plunder it, but kill those who opposed the surrender and reduce the rest of the garrison to bondage, leaving the inhabitants unharmed. If the Utopians find any of the inhabitants who recommended surrender, they share with them part of the property of those who have been condemned, and then divide the rest among the auxiliary troops. None of the Utopians themselves want any of the spoils.

When a war is ended, they charge the cost to the conquered, not to the friends for whom they undertook it. They take the indemnity either in the form of money, which they set aside for future use in war, or in the form of land, which produces a constant revenue of considerable amount. At the present time they draw this sort of revenue from many peoples, amounting with gradual increases from various sources to more than 700,000 ducats a year. They send some of their own citizens abroad as tax collectors to receive these revenues, with orders to live sumptuously and to conduct themselves like great personages. Even then much remains, which they are to bring home to their own treasury or which, as often happens, they lend to the people who already have it in hand, until it is needed at home. They seldom call it all in. They assign part of the lands as rewards to those whom they have urged to risk great dangers, such as I have mentioned.

If any prince has taken up arms and is preparing to invade their realm, they at once attack him in strength outside their own territory. For they do not willingly wage war on their own soil, and no necessity could force them to admit foreign auxiliaries to their island to aid them.

THE RELIGION OF THE UTOPIANS

There are different kinds of religion throughout the island, as well as in each city. Some worship the sun as a god, others the moon, and still others some one of the planets. Others worship some man pre-eminent in virtue or glory, not only as a god, but as the supreme god. But by far the greatest number of the Utopians, and among these the wisest, worship none of these. They think there is one unknown, eternal, infinite, and unknowable deity, transcending human comprehension and pervading the whole universe not physically but in virtue and power. Him they call Father of all. They acknowledge that from Him alone comes the beginning, increase, progress, change, and end of all things. They do not offer divine honors to any other god.

Though they hold different beliefs on other matters of religion, all the Utopians agree with their wiser sort in this, that there is only one supreme power, the Maker and Ruler of the universe, whom they all call in their native language Mithra. But they differ as to who he is; some think he is one god, others another. But whatever god each person regards as the chief god, they all agree in thinking that God is the very Being to whose power and majesty the supremacy over all things is attributed by universal consent.

By degrees all the Utopians are coming to forsake their various superstitions and to agree upon this one religion that seems to excel the others in reason. No doubt the other religions would have vanished long ago, had it not happened that whenever one of the Utopians who was planning to change his religion met with misfortune, the rest regarded it not as an accident but as something sent by a divinity as a punishment for the desertion of his worship.

We told them of the name, doctrine, manner of life, and miracles of Christ, and of the wonderful constancy of the many martyrs, who willingly sacrificed their blood to bring so many nations far and wide to Christianity. You will hardly believe with what favorably disposed minds they received this account, either because God secretly incited them or because this religion is most like the belief already very strong among them. I thought that they were also somewhat influenced by learning that Christ instituted community of goods and that this custom was still in practice among the most sincere of the Christians. Whatever the reason, many came over to our religion and were baptized. Two of our number had died and none of us four survivors, I regret to say, were priests, so though they received instruction in other matters they did not receive those sacraments which in our religion only priests can administer. But they understand them and long for them ardently. In fact, they argue vigorously with one another as to whether a man chosen from among them without the Pope's authorization would have the true character of a priest. Though they seemed determined to choose such a one, they had not chosen him at the time of my leaving.

Those among them that have not yet accepted the Christian religion do not restrain others from it nor abuse the converts to it. While I was there, only one man among the Christians was punished. This newly baptized convert, in spite of all our advice, was preaching in public on the Christian worship more zealously than wisely. He grew so heated that he not only put our worship before all others, but also condemned all other rites as profane and loudly denounced their celebrants as wicked and impious men fit for hell fire. After he had been preaching these things for a long time, they seized him. They convicted him not on a charge of disparaging their religion, but of arousing public disorder among the people, and sentenced him to exile. For they count it among their oldest institutions that no man shall be made to suffer for his religion.

In the early days King Utopus learned that before his coming the inhabitants had quarreled violently over religion. He found that it was easy to conquer them all, because the different sects in fighting for their country fought by themselves instead of together. Therefore after his victory he decreed that each man might follow whatever religion he wished and might try to persuade others to join it amicably and temperately and without bitterness toward others. If persuasion failed, a person was forbidden to use force or to indulge in wrangling. If anyone argued for his religion contentiously, he was to be punished by exile or bondage.

Utopus made this law partly for the sake of peace, which he saw was in danger of being completely destroyed by constant strife and implacable hatred, and partly for the sake of religion. He did not venture to make dogmatic decisions in regard to religion, perhaps from some idea that God likes and inspires a variety and multiplicity of worship. He deemed it foolish and insolent for anyone to try to make all men accept his own beliefs by force and by threats. If one religion is true and the others false, and if men use reason and moderation, he clearly foresaw that the truth would prevail by its own strength. But if men fight and riot, as evil and headstrong men will do, then the best and holiest religion in the world will be crowded out by the emptiest superstitions, like wheat choked by thorns and briars. So he imposed no one religion on his people, and left each man free to believe what he would, with one exception. He made a solemn and severe law against any who sink so far below the dignity of human nature as to think that the soul dies with the body, or that the universe is carried along by chance without an over-ruling providence.

The Utopians believe that after this life there are punishments for wickedness and rewards for virtue. They consider one who thinks otherwise as hardly a man, since he has degraded the human soul to the low level of a beast's body. Such a man they do not count fit for human society, for if he dares, he will scorn all its laws and customs. Who can doubt that a man who fears nothing but the law and apprehends nothing after death would secretly flout his country's laws or break them by force to satisfy his greed? Therefore no preferment is awarded to one with such views, and no magistracy or any public responsibility is entrusted to him. Instead, he is generally looked down upon as a man of worthless and sordid nature. Yet they do not punish such a man further, for they are persuaded that no one can make himself believe anything at will. Nor do they force him by threats to conceal his thoughts, and so open the door to deceit and lying, which they detest as the next thing to fraud. But they take care that he does not argue for his opinions, especially before the common people. They permit and even encourage him to discuss these matters with their priests and other serious men, in full confidence that finally his mad opinions will yield to reason.

There are others, in fact a considerable number, who go to the opposite extreme, and believe that the souls of animals are immortal, though not comparable with the human soul in excellence nor capable of as great happiness. These men are not thought to be bad or altogether lacking in reason, and their opinion is not discouraged.

Almost all the Utopians believe so firmly that man's happiness after death is endless, that they lament sickness but not death. They only mourn a man's death if they see that he parts with life reluctantly. This they take as a very bad sign, as if his soul dreaded death because of hopelessness or from some secret and guilty foreboding of impending punishment. The coming of a man who does not run gladly at the call, but is dragged off like a shirker, cannot be pleasing to God. They feel horror at such a death, and after carrying out the body in sorrow and with silent prayers to God mercifully to pardon the man's weakness, they bury the body in the earth. When a man dies cheerfully and full of good hope, they do not grieve, but follow the body singing, earnestly commending the man's soul to God. Then they cremate him reverently rather than sadly, and in the place where the funeral pyre was made, they set up a tombstone with the dead man's honors engraved upon it. When they return from the funeral, they relate his life and good deeds, and no part of his life is more frequently nor more gladly rehearsed than his cheerful death.

They think that remembering his good qualities is a powerful incitement to virtue among the living and the most pleasing honor to the dead. For they believe that the dead are present among us and hear the talk about themselves, though they are invisible through the dullness of human sight. They think that the dead, in keeping with their happy condition, can go where they want, and in affectionate loyalty visit those they loved and esteemed during their lives. They also believe that in good men these affections, like other good things, are increased rather than decreased after death, and that the dead come among the living observing their words and deeds. Consequently they enter into their undertakings all the more confidently because of their trust in such protectors. And they are deterred from secret wrong-doing by the belief that their forefathers are present.

They laugh at auguries and other superstitious forms of divination that are common among other nations. But they revere miracles which cannot flow from the powers of nature, looking on them as the works and witnesses of God. They say that such miracles have frequently occurred among them. Sometimes they have won safety and success amid great dangers and uncertainties through public prayers offered with assured confidence.

They hold that the careful observation of nature and the reflection on it and the reverence that arises from this is a kind of worship very pleasing to God.

Not a few among them are led by their religion to neglect learning, to pursue no sort of study, nor even to allow themselves any leisure, but are always busy about good works. They believe that their future happiness after death is increased by good works toward others. Some of them visit the sick, others mend roads, clean ditches, repair bridges, dig turf, gravel, and stones, fell and cut up trees, and bring wood, grain, and other things into the cities by wagon. They work for private citizens as well as the public, and do even more work than bondmen. They undertake willingly and cheerfully any work that is rough, hard, or dirty, or such as frightens away most people because it is heavy, loathsome, and discouraging. By this means they secure leisure for others while they themselves are continually at work. They take no pay, and they do not reprove others for their way of living. They do not boast of their own lives. The more they serve others, the more they are held in honor among all people.

These persons are of two kinds. The first are celibates, and abstain entirely from meat as well as from women, some of them from every sort of flesh whatsoever. They utterly reject the pleasures of this life as harmful; they eagerly and earnestly strive for the joys of the life to come, hoping soon to attain it by watches and severe toil. The other kind are no less eager to work, but they marry. They do not scorn the solace of marriage, and they feel that they owe toil to nature (to make nature productive) and children to their native land. They avoid no pleasure so long as it does not interfere with their labor. They enjoy meat because they think that by it they are made stronger for labor. The Utopians consider these the wiser men, but the other kind the holier ones. If any man claimed that he preferred celibacy to marriage and a hard life to an easy one on the grounds of reason, they would laugh at him. But since the ascetics claim to be moved to their way of life by religion, the Utopians look up to them and revere them. They are very careful to state anything concerning religion precisely, so they call these ascetic men *buthrescas* in their language, a term which may be translated as "men in religious orders."

Their priests are men of great holiness, and are therefore few in number. In fact not over thirteen are permitted in each city, one for each temple. If there is a war, seven of them go out with the army and others fill their places temporarily. When the war is over, each priest returns to his former place. Until the substitute priests succeed priests who die, they live as companions to the chief priest. For one priest is in authority over the others. The priests are chosen by secret popular vote, as are the other magistrates, in order to avoid strife. After election they are consecrated by the college of priests. They are in charge of all sacred affairs, they supervise worship, and they act as overseers of the people's conduct. It is a great disgrace for anyone to be summoned to them and taken to task for living a dishonorable life. The priests' duty is only to counsel and advise. The prince and the other magistrates correct and punish offenders, though the priests excommunicate those that are very bad. No form of punishment is more dreaded than this. It burdens the wrongdoer with infamy and torments him with religious fear. Not even his body is safe for long, for unless he speedily convinces the priests of his repentance, he will be arrested and punished by the senate for impiety.

The priests are the teachers of the boys and youths. Instruction in good manners and virtue is considered as important as instruction in learning. The priests make the greatest effort to inculcate sound beliefs and concepts into the malleable minds of the boys, in order to preserve the commonwealth. When such ideas have been deeply impressed, they stay with a man throughout his life and make him most valuable in preserving the well-being of the state, which only declines from the vices which arise from bad moral attitudes.

Women are not excluded from the priesthood, but are chosen less often, and only if they are elderly widows. The wives of the priests are the chief women in the whole country, except for the women priests.

No greater honor is paid to any magistrate among the Utopians than to the priests. Even if one of them does something criminal, he is not subject to any state trial. Instead the judgment is left to God and to his own conscience. They do not think it right to lay hands on any priest, no matter how bad he is, since a priest is specially dedicated to God as if he were a sacred offering. This custom they observe all the more easily because the priests are few in number and selected with such care. It rarely happens that a man chosen as a singularly good man and raised to such an honor wholly because of his character falls into corruption and vice. If such a thing should happen, for human nature is changeable, no great harm to the state is to be feared from their immunity, because priests are few in number and without any power except that arising from the respect paid them. They prefer to have few priests, lest the dignity of that order which they esteem so highly grow cheap if shared among many, and because they think it hard to find men equal to that dignity to which the ordinary virtues do not suffice to raise them.

Their priests are venerated as much among foreign nations as they are among themselves, as is very clear from the following custom. When their soldiers engage in battle, the priests of the Utopians kneel down not far away, wearing their sacred vestments. With hands uplifted to heaven, they pray first of all for peace, then for victory for themselves without much bloodshed on either side. And when the victory turns to their side, the priests run among their own battle lines and restrain the fury of their soldiers. If any of the enemy soldiers see these priests and call to them, that is enough to save their lives. And if they touch the garments of a priest, that will save their property from all injury. Their priests are so greatly reverenced and venerated among all the peoples in that part of the world, that they have preserved the Utopians from the fury of the enemy as often as they have saved the enemy from their own soldiers. Sometimes when the Utopian line of battle has been broken and all hope lost, and the enemy in fierce pursuit thirsting for slaughter and plunder, the priests have stopped the bloodshed, separated the troops, and made a fair peace. There is nowhere any tribe so fierce, cruel, and barbarous as not to hold their persons sacred and inviolable.

The Utopians celebrate the first and last days of each month as holidays. They divide the year into months, which they measure by the course of the moon, just as they measure the year by the circuit of the sun. The first day they call in their language the Cynemern, the last day the Trapemern, which may be translated as the first and the last festival day.

They have magnificent temples, built with great effort and able to hold a great many people. This is a necessity, since they have built so few of them. The temples are somewhat dark inside, not from any error in architecture, but by the advice of the priests, who think that in a strong light the thoughts are scattered, but in a rather dim light the thoughts are collected and devotion heightened.

Though there are many different religions among them, yet all these, no matter how different, agree in the main point, the worship of the one Divine Nature, as though they were all going toward one destination by different routes. So nothing is seen or heard in the temples which does not suit all their religions. Any rite that is peculiar to some one sect is celebrated in a private home, but the public worship is performed in such a way as not to interfere with the private rites. There are no images of God in their temples, so that everyone may conceive of God in any form he wishes. They do not call upon God by different names, but use only the name Mithra. However they may conceive of him, all alike agree in calling the one Divine Majesty by this name. They offer no prayers that will offend any sect.

They meet in their temples on the evening of the holiday which closes the month, and while still feasting they thank God for their good fortune during that month or year which is ending. On the next day, which is the first festival day of the new month, they meet in the morning in their temples to pray for the prosperous and happy outcome of their affairs in the ensuing month or year. On each last holiday, before going to the temple, wives fall on their knees before their husbands, children before their parents. They confess every misdeed or failure, and ask forgiveness for their offenses. Thus any cloud of domestic discord is removed, and they may engage in their devotions with a serene and untroubled mind. They hold it wrong to worship with a troubled conscience. If they are aware of hatred or anger in their hearts toward anyone, they do not presume to take part in the service until they have been reconciled and their feelings purified, for fear of some great and immediate punishment. In the temples the men and women are separated, the men going to the right, the women to the left. The men of each household seat themselves in front of the master of their household and the women in front of the mistress. In this way their behavior in public may be seen by those who manage and direct them at home. They take great care that younger and older may be seated here and there promiscuously. If the boys sat together, they might waste in childish foolery the time in which they ought to develope a religious dread of God, which is the greatest and almost the only incitement to virtue.

They do not offer animal sacrifices. They think that a kind god, who gives these creatures life, will not be pleased by their slaughter. They burn incense and scatter perfumes and offer wax candles, not with the thought that this profits the Divine Nature in any way, for not even prayers do that. But they think that this is a harmless sort of worship, and that men are somehow elevated by odors, lights, and ritual, and take part in divine worship with a more fervent spirit.

In the temple the people wear white, and the priest wears a varicolored robe that is marvelous in workmanship and appearance, but is not made of costly material. It is not interwoven with thread of gold nor set with precious stones, but is so skillfully inwrought with various kinds of feathers that the value of the workmanship could not be exceeded by the costliest materials. Moreover they say that certain mysteries are symbolized in the pattern of the feathers on the priestly vestments, the meaning of which is carefully handed down among the priests to remind them of God's benefits to men and their duties both to God and to one another.

As soon as the priest comes from the vestry in his robes, the people all prostrate themselves reverently on the ground with so deep a silence that the very sight strikes a certain dread, as though a divinity were actually present. After they have remained in this posture for some time, they rise at a sign from the priest. Then they sing hymns, accompanied by musical instruments different from those seen in our part of the world. Many of theirs are sweeter than ours, but some are much inferior. Without doubt they excel us in one thing: all their music, both vocal and instrumental, imitates and expresses the feelings and is well suited in sound to the occasion or subject. Whether the mood of the hymn is cheerful, pleading, troubled, sad, or angry, the music penetrates and inspires the minds of the hearers. Finally the priest and the people offer solemn prayers in a set form, so composed that what they all recite in unison each one applies to himself.

In these prayers each one acknowledges God to be the creator, ruler, and author of all good things, thanking Him for the many benefits received and in particular for the fact that through God's favor they have been born into this commonwealth, which is the happiest, and into this religion, which they hope is the truest. If they are mistaken in this, and if there be any kind of society or religion that is more acceptable to God, they pray that in His goodness He will reveal this to them, for they are ready to follow wherever he leads them. But if their social organization is the best and their religion is the truest, then they pray that He will make them steadfast therein and bring the rest of mankind to the same rules of life and the same concept of God, unless by His inscrutable will He prefers the present diversity of religions.

Then they pray that after an easy death God will receive each of them to Himself. They do not presume to set a time, how soon or how late their passing shall be. But if it may be wished for, without offense to His divine majesty, they pray to go to God soon, even though by the hardest death, rather than be kept away from Him longer by the most prosperous course of life! When this prayer has been finished, they bow again to the ground and after a little they rise again and go home to dinner. The rest of the day they spend in games and martial exercises.

Now I have described to you as truthfully as I could the structure of this commonwealth, which I think the best, and indeed the only one which can rightfully be called by that name. In other places where they speak of the common good, every man is looking out for his own good. But in Utopia where there is no private property and where they zealously pursue the public business, there the name commonwealth is doubly deserved. Elsewhere, even though the state is prosperous, most men know that they may die of hunger if they do not look out for themselves, and so they are forced to take care of themselves rather than other people. In Utopia where everything belongs to everybody, they know that if the public warehouses and granaries are full, no one will lack anything for his personal use.

Among them there is no mal-distribution of goods, nor is anyone poor and indigent. When no one owns anything, all are rich. What greater riches can there be than to live cheerfully and serenely, free from all anxieties, without worries about making a living and unvexed by the complaints of one's wife about money? No one has to worry about his son's being poor, or about his daughter's dowry. Each man's livelihood and happiness are secure, and the same is true of all his relations, his wife, sons, grandsons, great-grandsons, and the whole line of descendants that highborn men assume will follow them. Why should he look forward to less, since those who can no longer work are cared for as well as those who do?

How could anyone dare to compare the justice of the Utopians with that of other nations? If there is any trace of justice or equity among other nations, may I perish among them! What justice is there in this, that a nobleman, a goldsmith, a moneylender, or some other man who does nothing at all for a living or does something that is of no use to the public, lives a sumptuous and elegant life? In the meantime a servant, a driver, a blacksmith, or a farmer works as hard as a beast at labor so necessary that the commonwealth could not last a year without it. Yet they earn so poor a living and lead such miserable lives that their condition seems worse than that of draft animals. Beasts do not work so incessantly and do not live much worse—in fact they live better—and they have no worries about the future. But working men are burdened with barren and fruitless toil, and live in fear of want in their old age. Their daily wage is insufficient to support them for the present, so they can have no surplus to lay up for the future.

Is not a government unjust and ungrateful that squanders rich rewards on noblemen (as they are called), goldsmiths, and others that do not work but live only by flattery or by catering to useless pleasures? And is it just for a government to ignore the welfare of farmers, charcoal burners, servants, drivers, and blacksmiths, without whom the commonwealth could not exist at all? After their best years have been consumed by labor and they are worn out by age and sickness, they are still penniless, and the thankless state, unmindful of their many great services, rewards them with nothing but a miserable death. Furthermore the rich constantly try to whittle away something from the pitiful wages of the poor by private fraud and even by public laws. To pay so little to men who deserve the best from the state is in itself unjust, yet it is made "just" legally by passing a law.

So when I weigh in my mind all the other states which flourish today, so help me God, I can discover nothing but a conspiracy of the rich, who pursue their own aggrandizement under the name and title of the Commonwealth. They devise ways and means to keep safely what they have unjustly acquired, and to buy up the toil and labor of the poor as cheaply as possible and oppress them. When these schemes of the rich become established by the government, which is meant to protect the poor as well as the rich, then they are law. With insatiable greed these wicked men divide among themselves the goods which would have been enough for all.

And yet they are far short of the happiness of the Utopians, who have abolished the use of money, and with it greed. What evils they avoid! What a multitude of crimes they prevent! Everyone knows that frauds, thefts, quarrels, contentions, uprisings, murders, betrayals, and poisonings (evils which are commonly punished rather than checked by the severities of the law) would wither away if money were eradicated! Fear, anxiety, worry, care, toil, and sleepless nights would disappear at the same time as money! Even poverty, which seems to need money more than anything else for its relief, would vanish if money were gone.

To see this more clearly, consider this one example. Take some poor and unfruitful year in which hunger has carried off many thousands of men. If the barns of the rich were searched at the end of the year, I maintain that enough grain would be found to feed everyone, and to save those who died from the famine and from the plague caused by the famine. How easily the bare needs of life might be provided, if money, which is meant to procure us the necessities of life, did not itself deter us! Certainly rich men know this. They also know that it would be more practicable to provide the necessities of life for everyone than to supply superfluities for a few, and much better to eradicate our innumerable evils than to be burdened with great concentrations of wealth.

If that one monster pride, the first and foremost of all evils, did not forbid it, the whole world would doubtless have adopted the laws of the Utopians long before this, drawn on by a rational perception of what each man's true interest is or else by the authority of Christ our Saviour, who in His great wisdom knows what is best and in His loving kindness bids us do it. Pride measures her prosperity not by her own goods but by others' wants. Pride would not deign to be a goddess, if there were no inferiors she could rule and triumph over. Her happiness shines brightly only in comparison to others' misery, and their poverty binds them and hurts them the more as her wealth is displayed. Pride is the infernal serpent that steals into the hearts of men, thwarting and holding them back from choosing the better way of life.

Pride is far too deeply rooted in men's hearts to be easily torn out. I am glad, therefore, that the Utopians have achieved their social organization, which I wish all mankind would imitate. Their institutions give their commonwealth a moral and social foundation for living happy lives, and as far as man can predict, these institutions will last forever. Because they have rooted out ambition and strife along with other vices, they are in no danger of civil wars, which have ruined many states that seemed secure. And as long as they maintain sound institutions and domestic harmony, they can never be overcome by the envious rulers near by, who have often attempted their ruin in vain.

*   *   *

Thus Raphael finished speaking. I admit that not a few things in the manners and laws of the Utopians seemed very absurd to me: their way of waging war, their religious customs, as well as other matters, but especially the keystone of their entire system, namely, their communal living without the use of money. This one thing takes away all the nobility, magnificence, splendor, and majesty which public opinion commonly regards as the true ornaments of a nation. But I saw that Raphael was tired with talking, and I was not sure that he could bear contradiction in these matters. I remembered that he had spoken ill of certain men who feared they would not be thought wise unless they could find something to criticize in other men's opinions.

So with praise for the Utopian institutions and for his account of them, I took him by the hand and led him in to supper, adding that we would find some other time for considering these things more thoroughly and for talking with him in greater detail about them. I hope that such an opportunity may come some time. Meanwhile I cannot agree with everything that he said, though he was singularly well informed and also highly experienced in worldly affairs. Yet I must confess that there are many things in the Utopian Commonwealth that I wish rather than expect to see followed among our citizens.

Bibliography

WORKS ON UTOPIA

Karl Kautsky, *Thomas More and His Utopia,* trans. H. J. Stenning, New York, 1927.

H. W. Donner, *Introduction to Utopia,* London, 1945.

Russell Ames, *Citizen Thomas More and His Utopia,* Princeton, 1948.

Jack H. Hexter, *More's Utopia: The Biography of an Idea,* Princeton, 1952.

Edward L. Surtz, *The Praise of Pleasure; Philosophy, Education, and Communism in More's Utopia,* Cambridge, Mass., 1957.

Edward L. Surtz, *The Praise of Wisdom; A Commentary on the Religious and Moral Problems and Backgrounds of St. Thomas More's Utopia,* Chicago, 1957.

ENGLISH TRANSLATIONS OF UTOPIA

J. H. Lupton, *The Utopia of Sir Thomas More,* Oxford, 1895. (Includes the Latin original, the Robinson translation of 1551, and important notes).

J. C. Collins, *Sir Thomas More's Utopia,* Oxford, 1904. (The Robinson translation with very full notes.)

Edward Surtz, ed., *St. Thomas More: Utopia,* New Haven, 1964. (A revision of a 1923 translation by G. C. Richards.)

LIVES OF SIR THOMAS MORE

William Roper, *The Life of Sir Thomas More,* ed. E. V. Hitchcock, Oxford, 1935.

Nicholas Harpsfield, *The Life and Death of Sir Thomas More,* ed. E. V. Hitchcock, London, 1932.

R. W. Chambers, *Thomas More,* London, 1935.

HISTORICAL BACKGROUND

P. S. Allen, *The Age of Erasmus,* Oxford, 1914.

A. F. Pollard, *Wolsey,* London, 1929.

G. R. Elton, *England under the Tudors,* London and New York, 1955.